A Unifying Framework for Structured Analysis and Design Models:
An Approach using Initial Algebra Semantics and Category Theory

Cambridge Tracts in Theoretical Computer Science

Managing Editor Professor C.J. van Rijsbergen, Department of Computing Science, University of Glasgow

Titles in the series

1. G. Chaitin *Algorithmic Information Theory*
2. L.C. Paulson *Logic and Computation*
3. M. Spivey *Understanding Z*
4. G. Revesz *Lambda Calculus, Combinators and Logic Programming*
5. A. Ramsay *Formal Methods in Artificial Intelligence*
6. S. Vickers *Topology via Logic*
7. J-Y. Girard, Y. Lafont & P. Taylor *Proofs and Types*
8. J. Clifford *Formal Semantics & Pragmatics for Natural Language Processing*
9. M. Winslett *Updating Logical Databases*
10. K. McEvoy & J.V. Tucker (eds) *Theoretical Foundations of VLSI Design*
11. T.H. Tse *A Unifying Framework for Structured Analysis and Design Models*
12. G. Brewka *Nonmonotonic Reasoning*
13. G. Smolka *Logic Programming over Polymorphically Order-Sorted Types*
15. S. Dasgupta *Design Theory and Computer Science*
17. J.C.M. Baeten (ed) *Applications of Process Algebra*
18. J.C.M. Baeten & W.P. Weijland *Process Algebra*

A Unifying Framework for Structured Analysis and Design Models:
An Approach using Initial Algebra Semantics and Category Theory

T.H. Tse, M.B.E.
University of Hong Kong

The right of the
University of Cambridge
to print and sell
all manner of books
was granted by
Henry VIII in 1534.
The University has printed
and published continuously
since 1584.

CAMBRIDGE UNIVERSITY PRESS

Cambridge

New York   Port Chester   Melbourne   Sydney

CAMBRIDGE UNIVERSITY PRESS
Cambridge, New York, Melbourne, Madrid, Cape Town, Singapore, São Paulo, Delhi

Cambridge University Press
The Edinburgh Building, Cambridge CB2 8RU, UK

Published in the United States of America by Cambridge University Press, New York

www.cambridge.org
Information on this title: www.cambridge.org/9780521117876

First published 1991
This digitally printed version 2009

A catalogue record for this publication is available from the British Library

ISBN 978-0-521-39196-2 hardback
ISBN 978-0-521-11787-6 paperback

To Teresa

CONTENTS

Chapter 4. An Initial Algebra Framework for Unifying the Structured Models

Chapter 5. A Functorial Framework for Unifying the Structured Models

Chapter 6. The Identification of Unstructuredness

Chapter 7. A Prototype System to Implement the Unifying Framework

Chapter 8. Conclusion

Bibliography

Preface

Structured analysis and design methodologies have been recognized as a popular and powerful tool in information systems development. A complex system can be specified in a top-down and graphical fashion, enabling practitioners to visualize the target systems and communicate with users much more easily than by means of conventional methods. As a matter of fact, the structured methodologies have been designed by quite a number of distinct authors, each employing a number of models which vary in their graphical outlook. Different models are found to be suitable for different stages of a typical systems life cycle. A specification must be converted from one form to another during the development process. Unfortunately, however, the models are only derived from the experience of the authors. Little attempt has been made in proposing a formal framework behind them or establishing a theoretical link between one model and another.

A unifying framework is proposed in this book. We define an initial algebra of structured systems, which can be mapped by unique homomorphisms to a DeMarco algebra of data flow diagrams, a Yourdon algebra of structure charts and a Jackson algebra of structure texts. We also find that the proposed initial algebra as well as the structured models fit nicely into a functorial framework. DeMarco data flow diagrams can be mapped by a free functor to terms in the initial algebra, which can then be mapped to other notations such as Yourdon structure charts by means of forgetful functors. The framework also provides a theoretical basis for manipulating incomplete or unstructured specifications through refinement morphisms.

Since flow diagrams are used for problem analysis and communicating with users during early systems development, they are problem-oriented and are not necessarily structured. Some detection mechanism must be available for us to identify unstructuredness in the flow diagrams before we can convert them into structure charts or any other structured models. As a further illustration of the theoretical usefulness of our formal framework, we have derived a single criterion which is necessary and sufficient to identify unstructuredness in tasks. Namely, a connected task is unstructured if and only if there exist partially overlapping skeletons. As an illustration of the practical usefulness of our framework, we have developed a prototype system to implement the structured tasks. It enables users to draw a hierarchy of DeMarco data flow diagrams, review them to an appropriate level of detail, and zoom in/zoom out to lower/higher levels when required. It stores them internally as structured tasks, and transforms them automatically into Yourdon structure charts and Jackson structure texts.

This work originated from my Ph.D. research at the London School of Economics, University of London. I would like to express my sincere thanks to my supervisors Professor Ian Angell and Professor Ronald Stamper (now with the University of Twente) for their guidance throughout the doctoral programme. I am particularly indebted to Professor Joseph Goguen of the University of Oxford for his most encouraging comments and suggestions right from the very beginning of the project, and his endless advices on how to transform the thesis into the present work. I am grateful also to my external examiners Professor Bernie Cohen of the University of Surrey (now with Rex Thompson and Partners) and Professor John Campbell of University College London for their fair evaluation of the research. In addition, I will not forget the contributions of my former supervisor Professor Frank Land, now with the London Business School, without whose motivation this project would not have started in the first place.

Special thanks are due to Dr Haya Freedman of the Department of Mathematics, London School of Economics, for her knowledge base on initial algebra and category theory, to Mr Daniel Pong, now with the Bank of Montreal, Canada, for his technical assistance on requirements specification languages, and to Professor Francis Chin and other colleagues at the University of Hong Kong for their continuous interactions and support. My thanks should also go to Dr Peter Breuer and Dr Paritosh Pandya of the University of Oxford, Professor Rod Burstall of the University of Edinburgh, Dr Derek Coleman of Hewlett-Packard Laboratories, Professor Joe Davis of Indiana University, Professor Dr Hartmut Ehrig of Technische Universitaet Berlin, Professor Jim Emery of the University of Pennsylvania, Dr Kit Grindley of Price Waterhouse, Dr Don Sannella of the University of Bremen and Dr Sami Zahran of ICL Dataskil for their encouraging feedbacks.

The research would not have been successful without the study leaves granted by the University of Hong Kong, a Commonwealth Academic Staff Scholarship and a CICHE Visitorship at the University of London, a SERC Visiting Fellowship at the University of Oxford, a Fellowship of the International Conference on Information Systems, a Grant from the International Conference on Software Engineering, a Hong Kong and China Gas Co. Research Grant and a University of Hong Kong Research and Conference Grant.

Finally, I would like to mention a word of 謝謝 to my wife, children and other members of the family for their patience, love and care throughout the duration of the project.

LIST OF TABLES AND FIGURES

List of Tables

List of Figures

1 Introduction

The specifier constructs a theory and attempts to refute it (hypothetico-deductive) while the knowledge engineer assembles a mass of empirical rules whose verisimilitude is unquestioned (empirico-deductive). The systems engineer, meanwhile, takes the utilitarian approach: if it works, use it.

—Bernard Cohen et al. (1986)

There are existing formalisms for description ... which are clear and well-understood, but lack the richness typical in descriptions which people find useful. They can serve as a universal basis for description but only in the same sense that a Turing machine can express any computation.

—Terry Winograd (1979)

Structured analysis and design methodologies have been recognized as the most popular tools in information systems development (Colter 1982). They are widely accepted by practising systems developers because of the top down nature of the methodologies and the graphical nature of the tools. A complex systems specification can be decomposed into a modular and hierarchical structure which is easily comprehensible. They enable practitioners to visualize the target systems and to communicate with users much more easily than conventional methods.

As a matter of fact, the structured methodologies have been designed by quite a number of distinct authors, each employing a number of models which vary in their in graphical outlook. These include data flow diagrams (DeMarco 1978, Gane and Sarson 1979, McMenamin and Palmer 1984, Weinberg 1980), Jackson structure diagrams, Jackson structure texts (Jackson 1975), system specification diagrams, system implementation diagrams (Cameron 1986, Jackson 1983), Warnier/Orr diagrams (Orr 1977) and structure charts (Page-Jones 1988, Yourdon and Constantine 1979).

Different structured models have been found to be suitable for different situations depending on the characteristics of user requirements, the emphasis and the stage of development. In other words, we need more than one of these models during the development process of a typical system. If we provide practitioners with a computer-aided means of mapping one model to another, the efficiency of systems development can be greatly improved. Unfortunately, however, the models are only derived from the experience of the authors. In spite of the popularity of these models, relatively little work has been done in providing a theoretical framework for them. As a result, the transition from one model to another, although recommended by most authors, is arbitrary and only done manually. Automatic validation and development aids tend to be *ad hoc* and model-dependent.

On the other hand, many attempts have already been made to computerize the systems development environment. Some better known examples are ADS/SODA, EDDA, ISDOS, SAMM and SREM. Most of these approaches, however, are developed independently of existing structured analysis and design models. As pointed out in Davis (1982) and Martin (1983, 1984), practitioners are rather hesitant to use such new tools because they involve an unfamiliar formal language.

To solve the problem, we should not be designing yet another formal language from scratch. Instead, we must recognize the popularity of existing methodologies and apply mathematical theory to support them. In this book, we propose a unifying framework behind the structured models, approaching the problem from the viewpoints of initial algebra and category theory. We hope it will provide further insight for software engineers into systems development methodologies, guidelines for implementors of advanced CASE tools, and will open up a range of applications and problems for theoretical computer scientists.

In Chapter 2 of the book, we review the desirable features of a systems development environment. In Chapter 3, we examine the features of five related projects, thus comparing the structured models with other tools which have a better formal foundation but are less popular. In the initial algebra framework discussed in Chapter 4, we define a term algebra of structured systems, which can be mapped by unique homomorphisms to a DeMarco algebra of data flow diagrams, a Yourdon algebra of structure charts and a Jackson algebra of structure texts. In Chapter 5, we find that the proposed term algebra as well as the DeMarco, Yourdon and Jackson notations fit nicely into a category-theoretic framework. DeMarco data flow diagrams can be mapped to term algebras through free functors. Conversely, specifications in term algebras can be mapped to other notations such as Yourdon structure charts by means of functors. The framework also provides a theoretical basis for manipulating incomplete or unstructured specifications through refinement morphisms.

A further illustration of the theoretical usefulness of the concept of tasks is given in Chapter 6. Since flow diagrams are used for problem analysis and communicating with users during early systems development, they are problem-oriented and are not necessarily structured. Some detection mechanism must be available for us to identify any unstructuredness in the flow diagrams before we can convert them into structure charts or any other structured models. We prove that a single criterion is necessary and sufficient for identifying unstructured tasks. An illustration of the practical useful-ness is given in Chapter 7, where we discuss a prototype system to implement the structured tasks. It enables users to draw a hierarchy of DeMarco data flow diagrams, review them to an appropriate level of detail, and zoom in/zoom out to lower/higher levels when required.

The project has been presented in Computer Science and Information Systems journals and conferences (see, for example, Tse 1986, 1987a, 1987b, 1987c, 1988). Feedbacks on our approach are favourable and encouraging.

2 Desirable Features of Systems Development Environments

2.1 INTRODUCTION

In the early days of stored program computers, the cost of software made up a mere 15 per cent of the total cost of information systems. But software cost has been escalating ever since, and is currently estimated to be over 80 per cent of the total (Boehm 1976), as illustrated in Figure 2.1. It is more alarming to note that more than two-thirds of the money is spent on the maintenance of existing software and only one-third on new developments.

In view of the escalation in software cost, research workers have been trying to improve on the languages used in systems specifications and to design development environments to support these languages. Quite a number of surveys on specification languages and their supporting environments have already been published. Some notable examples are Colter (1984), Jones (1979), Rock-Evans (1987), Wasserman

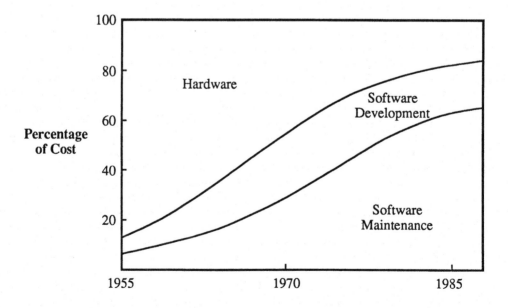

Figure 2.1 Hardware and Software Cost Trends

(1983) and Yau and Tsai (1986). Most of the authors (not excluding the present author (Tse and Pong 1982)) propose in the papers a list of desirable features of specification languages and/or development environments so as to provide a basis for judgement. One must confess that it is virtually impossible to invent yet another list of desirable features which would be better than those already proposed. Instead, we shall in this chapter consolidate the features already suggested by various authors and present them in the context of an engineering process. In the next chapter, we shall then use the proposed features as the basis to examine some of the established research in specification languages and their supporting environments.

Information systems development can be conceived as an engineering process. A graphical representation is shown in Figure 2.2. We must first of all build a model, which is a small-scaled abstract representation of the real world. All unnecessary details in the physical world which are irrelevant to the engineering process are removed. If the resulting model is still too complex, further abstractions may be necessary, until the problem is reduced to a manageable size. The model is then analysed and manipulated until a feasible solution is found. In engineering, diagrams and mathematics are often used because they have been found to be more suitable for manipulation than verbal descriptions. One representation may have to be transformed into another so that the most appropriate model for a given analysis can be used. When we solve an engineering problem, for instance, we may convert diagrams into equations or vice versa. Finally, if the abstract solution is accepted by the customer, a construction phase turns it into a real system.

A systems specification for the engineering process is important for several reasons:

(a) It serves as a communication medium between the user and the systems developer. It represents in a systematic fashion the current state of the real world, its problems and its future requirements.

(b) It enables the systems developer to turn real world problems into other forms which are more manageable in terms of size, complexity, human understanding and computer processability.

(c) It serves as the basis for the design, implementation, testing and maintenance of the target system.

In order for a systems specification to be useful for the entire engineering process, the specification language and its supporting environment must have the following features to cater for the respective stages:

2.2 ABSTRACTION OF THE REAL WORLD

A systems specification language is the medium for users to make a model of the real world and specify its problems and requirements. It is the bridge between a development environment and the users, including systems analysts, designers and end users. We must ensure that this interface is suitable to all concerned. The usual marketing

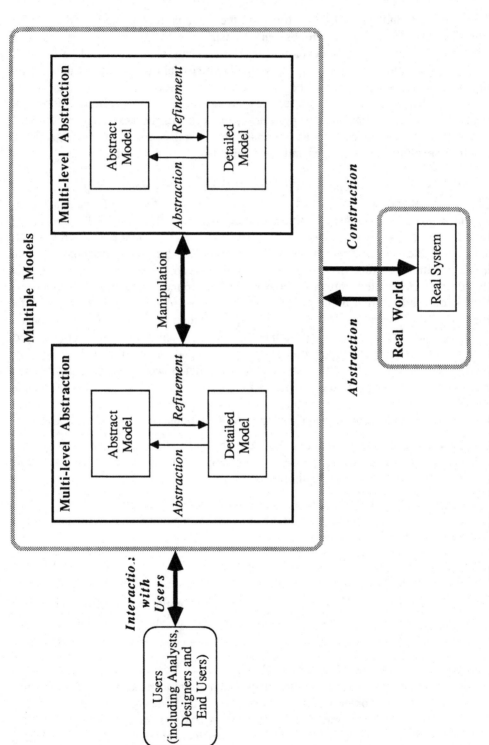

Figure 2.2   Schematic Concept of an Engineering Process

phrase ''user-friendliness'' is a bit too vague to act as a useful guide. Instead, we consider it essential for the systems specification language and its supporting environment to have the following properties:

2.2.1 User Familiarity of the Specification Language

It would be difficult for users to employ an entirely new specification language because of several reasons:

(a) There is an inertial effect from the point of view of users. They are not willing to try new methodologies which are not familiar, especially those involving formal languages.

(b) From the management point of view, a methodology which has been well-tested and which is being taught in various universities and polytechnics tends to be more acceptable than a newly proposed technique. It is easier to recruit staff members who are trained and experienced in an established method. It will be easier to maintain standards if the same methodology is used throughout the company. Managers in general find it safer to be old-fashioned than to try the latest innovation and regret afterwards.

When we propose a new systems development environment, therefore, we should not be inventing an entirely new language, with the hope that it will turn out to be the best in the world. Instead, we should try to use a currently available specification language which has most of the desirable features and, more importantly, has proven popularity among practitioners.

2.2.2 Language Style

To facilitate the automatic processing of a systems specification, it may be thought that the language used must be formal and mathematical in nature. A systems specification in a formal language, unfortunately, will be very difficult for users to understand. As pointed out in Davis (1982) and Martin (1983, 1984), practising systems analysts are very hesitant to such languages. Instead, the language must be easy to learn and easy to use. It must be close to the language employed by users in their respective domains of application. It must be precise and concise, or in other words, clear and to the point. Let us list out the possible classes of languages in order to arrive at some reasonable choice.

(a) *Textual language:* When we consider the use of a textual language for systems specification, we may like either a natural language or a more formal program-like language. There is little doubt that natural languages provide a better means of persuasion and more freedom of expression, especially in the early stages of systems development when a certain degree of uncertainty is involved. It is also more natural to the average end user and hence improves the user-understanding of a new situation. (The current book, for example, can only be written in a natural language, supplemented by graphics and other formal textual languages.)

Research workers in artificial intelligence, however, are still trying very hard to make natural language understood by computer systems, and hence it is currently impossible to find a development environment which supports specifications based on a natural language.

On the other hand, a specification in a natural language may cause ambiguities, since it may be interpreted differently by different people. As pointed out by DeMarco (1978) and others, standard English prose is not suitable even for systems specifications which are processed manually. Languages with a better defined syntax and slightly more restrictive semantics would therefore be preferred. These languages are more formal in nature and resemble a programming language or a mathematical language.

(b) *Graphical language:* It is generally agreed that graphical representation of complex material is much more comprehensible than its textual counterpart, because

(i) Graphics is more natural in giving users an intuitive picture of complex structures such as hierarchical organizations or parallelisms.

(ii) Graphics has two dimensions while text has only one dimension. This gives an additional degree of freedom in presentation.

It should be noted, however, that graphical languages with too many symbols are not necessarily comprehensible to end users. The graphics-based language must use only a relatively small number of easily understood symbols and conventions.

(c) *Hybrid language:* It is often impractical to define a specification only in terms of a single graphical or textual language. For example, although graphical languages are better than textual languages in presenting an overview of a complex situation, textual languages are regarded as better tools for detailed description. We need a language which exists in more than one format. A reasonable subset of the specification, at least at the higher levels of abstraction, must exist in both textual and graphical forms. The specification must be convertible from one form to another so that users, analysts, designers, implementors and managers can communicate effectively. A person needs only review the version most appropriate to his understanding and his needs. A formal one-to-one correspondence must be maintained among the various syntaxes of the specification language, so that there will not be any error or dispute.

2.2.3 Multi-level Abstraction

As suggested in Yeh and Zave (1980), complexity is the main barrier to the understanding of system problems. A systems specification language must therefore provide a means of improving the conceptual clarity of the problems. A hierarchical framework should be provided by the specification language so that users can visualize a target system more easily. It enables users to start conceptualizing the system at the highest level of abstraction, and then continue steadily downwards for further levels of details. It allows users to distinguish those parts of the target system relevant to a given context from those which are not. Such a top-down approach frees users from embarking on unnecessary details at a time when they should only be concerned with an overall view of the target system. On the other hand, it also allows certain parts of a system to be investigated in detail when other parts are not yet defined.

To enable users to relate a specification with real life problems, the specification language must help them to refine the target system in a natural way. Target subsystems should be as self-contained as possible. The interfaces between any two subsystems should be kept to a minimum but defined explicitly. This will reduce complexity, avoid misunderstanding, and make it possible for two subsystems to be analysed further by two different persons. System modules created this way can be reusable common components which are independent of the parent modules that call them. Furthermore, mechanisms should be build into the development environment to help users to check whether each refinement step is logically valid, so that each group of child modules exactly replaces the relevant parent module.

2.2.4 Feedback to Users
One criterion for a good development environment is that it must help its user to visualize the specified requirements and compare them with his actual needs. Such feedback has a positive psychological effect on the user, much to his personal satisfaction. Feedback to users can be achieved in several ways:

(a) *Interactive graphics input:* Since a systems analyst is usually analysing and designing a complex system in a top down and iterative manner, the development environment must allow him to review the specification and to add in further details interactively. Preferably, a user-friendly input tool supporting interactive graphics should be available so that he can have either have an overview of the target system or go into whatever level of details required. The graphics entered should then be convertible into a formal language for later stages of systems development.

(b) *Generation of documentation and graphics:* If the development environment cannot accept graphics interactively and turn it into a formal language, then we have to accept the systems specification in a textual language. In this case, the environment should convert the textual input into graphical output for users to verify and make corrections if necessary. Furthermore, if the textual language is mathematical or program-like, as is often the case, it will be compact and difficult to read. It would also be useful for the language processor to generate English-like narrative documentation to ease user-understanding. Other types of documentation, such as cross-reference tables and graphical summaries, should also be generated for users to check or simply to help consolidate their thoughts.

(c) *Prototyping:* Although it has been postulated that a specification must be complete in all aspects (Waters 1979), it would be quite inefficient if we have to wait for all information to be available before starting the development of a system. Users may not be able to completely specify their requirements at an early stage without a "feel" of the target system. A systems development environment should therefore tolerate incompleteness and allow users to partially specify their needs. A prototyping mechanism should then compile it into a preliminary system and hence provide the necessary feedback to users. Default options should also be allowed to simplify lower level specification processes, such as the designing of screen, report or file layouts. Given the prototype output, users can then refine their requirements through modifications and/or provision of additional details. Furthermore, it has been found that prototyping compares favourably with other methodologies for the detection of defects (Jones 1979).

2.2.5 Modifiability

The specification should be structured in such a way that parts of the target system can easily be modified to cater for new user needs, technological updates and/or other changes in the outside world. Such modifications should not necessarily be done by the original specifier but can be performed by anyone who is assigned the task.

2.3 MANIPULATION OF REPRESENTATIONS

2.3.1 Tools for Manipulation

(a) *Formalism:* In order to eliminate the problems of ambiguity during the construction and implementation of a target system, the systems specification must be expressible in a precise notation with unique interpretation. A formal framework should therefore be present. It will help to reduce the probability of ambiguities and misunderstanding. At the same time, automated tools based on the formal framework can be used to validate the syntactic consistency of the specification. Furthermore, given the complexity and scope of present day systems, manual development methods are highly ineffective. The construction process can be computer-aided more easily if a formal framework is present.

(b) *Mathematical rigour:* Software engineering, as it is being practised at the present moment, lacks any theoretical background and is seen by many as a black art (Cohen *et al.* 1986). In other engineering disciplines, such as mechanical or electrical engineering, the engineers can provide users with a guaranteed degree of confidence by supporting practice with theory, thereby allowing the production process to be subject to formal scrutiny. The engineer who supervises the construction of aeroplanes or electrical appliances, for instance, can proudly put his name on the final products, ensuring that they have been developed according to user specifications and free from errors and omissions. On the other hand, it is not in general possible for a software engineer or systems developer to do so (Parnas 1985). To solve this problem, the systems development process must be supported by theory, so that the correctness of implementation can be proved and verified against user requirements. We must ensure that the specification language is supported by a mathematical foundation so that it can be mapped to the appropriate theory when required.

The applications of formalism and mathematical rigour in the manipulation of the models and the construction of the real system are of such a vital importance that they will be elaborated further in the next sections.

2.3.2 Transformation

(a) *Support of different development notations:* It has been found that different models are needed for different development situations depending on the characteristics of user requirements (Sanden 1989, Shigo *et al.* 1980), the emphasis (Colter 1982) and the stage of development (Lauber 1982). For example, a model in the form of a tree structure may be employed to give users an overview of the target system. Another model showing algorithmic details may be more appropriate for the construction of the system. A third model in a mathematical form may be used for proving the correctness of implementation. Thus, specifications may have to be transformed from one style or notation to another. This raises the problem of determining whether the models are in fact equivalent in semantics, and is another reason why the models must be supported by mathematical rigour.

(b) *Transparency of formalism:* In order to support the manipulation and construction phases of the engineering process, a systems specification would probably consist of a substantial amount of formalism or jargon not fully understood by end users and their management. The formal and mathematical aspects of the specification language must be transparent to users because most people who are not mathematically trained will feel infuriated and shut off if they are presented with a list of Greek and Hebrew symbols. A unified mathematical framework must, however, be present in the language so that we can guarantee a one-to-one correspondence between the graphical side and the textual side of the same language. Otherwise it would be impossible to ensure, for example, that a hierarchical chart presented to the end user is the same as the algorithmic description read by the implementor.

2.3.3 Validation
Studies have shown that the cost of correcting an error after implementation is 50 to 1000 times that of correcting the same error during systems specification (Boehm 1983). It would be more economical and effective, therefore, if errors could be pinpointed and removed at the initial stage. For a large system, however, the specification may be very complex, and hence checking the correctness of its syntax manually may prove to be an impractical task. The development environment should

provide a mechanism for the early detection of design defects. Furthermore, even after implementation, when parts of the requirements need to be changed, the correctness of the modified specification must be confirmed again. A major function of the development environment is therefore to validate the syntax of the specification whenever the needs arise. We can separate the validation function into two areas.

(a) *Syntactic consistency:* The arguments for checking the syntactic consistency of a systems specification has been known for a long time. (See Fergus (1969), for example.) The development environment should be able to detect the following inconsistencies:

   (*i*)   Discrepancies between different parts of the specification;

   (*ii*) Parts of the requirement which have been referred to but not specified;

   (*iii*) If a specification is presented in the form of a structured hierarchy of modules, any conflict between a parent module and the corresponding child modules.

   Consistency checks are especially important when a large number of people are of a system.

(b) *Continuity:* In information systems, we are very much concerned about the flow of information from one source to another and the conversion of data from one form to another. We must make sure that

   (*i*)   Data items must have been input from a source or derived from other data items;

   (*ii*) Data items input or derived must be traceable to some use or destination;

   (*iii*) Data items must not be defined in circle;

   (*iv*) Data items used in a subsystem must not depend implicitly on data items outside the subsystem.

   Precedence analysis is required to check the continuity of data flows (Waters 1977).

(c) *User verification:* Direct verification* by users is another useful means of validating a specification. It is quite different from syntactic consistency checks performed internally by the system because, in the latter case, we are not able to find out whether the specification actually meets the requirements of the real world.

---

* The term "verification" is used in information systems to mean asking users to check whether the specification satisfies their needs. It should not be confused with the notion of "proof of correctness" as used by computer scientists.

Thus feedback must be provided to users for possible corrections. Methods of achieving this include generation of documentation, generation of cross references, generation of graphics and prototyping. In essence, these are similar in nature to the techniques discussed in Section 2.2.4 and will not be duplicated here.

2.3.4 Independence of Design and Implementation

A specification must be independent of the design and implementation of the target system. It should be behaviour-oriented, and support a logical system organization rather than a physical system organization. The specification must be open-ended in terms of implementation, rather than imposing a specific design choice such as the algorithms, files or databases to be used. It should not depend on the proposed hardware or other resources that are subject to change. It must not cause any obstacle to the introduction of new technologies.

2.4 CONSTRUCTION OF A REAL SYSTEM

2.4.1 Computability

Although program generation is an impossible task for the general case in computer science, the feasibility of code generation for information systems from appropriate specifications is well-known (Biggerstaff 1979, Hamilton and Zeldin 1983, Martin 1984). Information systems differ from other systems in two aspects:

- In information systems, the number of derivations (or computations) is usually small when compared with the number of transportations (or input/output) of data items. The processes involved are mainly "data driven", such as data capture, maintenance of files or databases, user enquiries and production of reports.

- User requirements are not absolutely non-procedural, because most users would like to preserve some of the ways in which things are being done manually. Thus the requirements specifications do spell out procedures to a certain extent.

Unlike the designer of algorithms in computer science, therefore, the software engineer for information systems is more interested in solving the problems of input/output bottlenecks and file access times.

(a) *File design and optimization:* During the physical design phase, a software engineer for information systems has to design files or databases to suit the given hardware environment and processing requirements. He is faced with an over-abundance of choices, which grow exponentially with the complexity of the system and become unmanageable to the human mind. The development environment, in order to produce better file and database design, should include optimization modules. There are three approaches available.

  (i) *Simulation models:* Simulation techniques were mainly used in the earlier models for evaluating file organizations (Cardenas 1973). Since each model assumes a specific file structure, it is not possible to obtain an overall optimum unless several models are run and compared. Because of the increasing number of file structures available, such a method would either be very limited in scope or take infinite time to run.

(*ii*) *Analytical models:* The problem of physical file and database design can be expressed in mathematical programming terms. Thus, given constraints such as hardware configuration and probabilistic details of storage data, we want to determine such factors as file or database structure, access method, overflow mechanism and so on, so that the cost of data retrieval and maintenance, expressed as a function of response time and storage space, will be minimized. We note, however, that the problem has the following characteristics:

- For a given set of factors, the cost can be determined analytically, but is a non-linear function of the factors.

- For realistic situations, the number of factors is very large.

- Furthermore, each of the factors allows a large number of discrete choices.

The minimization problem therefore becomes one in non-linear integer programming with a large number of variables. Yao (1977) simplified the problem by concentrating only on the average characteristics of file organizations based on a single analytical model. The number of variables then becomes manageable. Using this as a first approximation, the number of subsequent choices will be limited. The detailed structures of the files or databases can then be worked out by simulation. One drawback of this method is that first approximations based on average characteristics can be far from optimal, so that fine tuning of such estimates may only produce a local optimum. Alternatively, we can use other techniques such as the approximation of an integer programming model by a continuous model, and the method of branch and bound to reduce the number of searches to a manageable size.

(*iii*) *Heuristics:* Some researchers have derived heuristic rules from mathematical models (Severance and Duhne 1976, Severance and Carlis 1977). Such rules can be implemented into the development environment for a near-optimal file or database design.

(*b*) *Process design and optimization:* In information systems, as we have noted earlier, we are concerned about the design of processes such that the transportational aspect is optimized. Transportation volume can be reduced as follows (Alter 1979, Severance and Lohman 1976):

(*i*)   *Vertical aggregation of processes:* Two sequential processes having a file as an intermediate buffer may be combined to reduce input/output volume.

(*ii*)   *Horizontal aggregation of processes:* Processes reading the same file may be combined to reduce the input volume.

(*iii*)   *Aggregation of files:* Files generated by the same process may be combined to reduce the output volume.

(*iv*)   *Use of differential files:* Data items having different frequencies of access are candidates for separation into two files.

Given the large number of possibilities of aggregating and separating files and processes, the development environment is faced with the task of selecting the optimal one. It is even more difficult in this case to apply the mathematical programming models discussed in Section (*a*) above.

Alter (1979) proposes the use of an iterative method. The problem is divided into two phases: file optimization and process optimization. An initial value is input to the first phase to trigger off a search for an optimal file design. The result is input to the second phase in search for an optimal process design. The latter then goes back to the first phase for an improvement of the files. The processes are repeated until any more improvement becomes insignificant. Within each phase, we can either make use of mathematical programming, or build a smaller iterative loop. Alter, for instance, suggests the latter, making use of the steepest ascent method.

Alternatively, heuristic rules derived from mathematical models can also be used to find a quick and near-optimal solution.

2.4.2 Verification of Implementation

A specification can be seen as a contract between the designer and the implementor. We must have an independent means of ascertaining whether an implementor has fulfilled such a contract. This can be done in two ways:

(*a*) *Traceability:* Suitable cross-referencing mechanisms should be provided in the systems specification language to support tracing the consistency between the specified and the target systems. Information in the systems specification should be traceable to elements in the final design and implementation. This enables us to verify that all the functions and constraints specified are actually addressed by the developed system. It also ensures that operations in the final system are attributed to requirements made in the original specification. Furthermore, the tracing mechanism should tolerate incomplete or dummy modules, so that partially completed systems can be traced, hence allowing a top-down approach to implementation.

(b) *Proof of correctness:* A systems specification serves to state precisely the requirements and objectives the target system is to satisfy. It defines what is required of the system. The programs in the system is a set of procedures to attain the required result. They spell out how the results can be obtained. As systems are becoming more and more complex, it is no longer possible to rely solely on test data to verify whether the implemented version behaves according to the specification. Test data can only be used to detect the presence of anomalies in a system, but cannot be used to prove the absence of such anomalies. Formal and mathematical methods, often known as proofs of correctness, can be used to predict the behaviours of the programs independently of how they are written, and verify that they agree with what is required.

Unfortunately, correctness proof techniques may not be practical in large information systems because they would be very difficult and expensive to implement. As a result, such techniques are applied only in special cases such as safety critical systems and VLSI, where the cost (economic or otherwise) of an error would be enormous.

2.5 CONCLUSION

The desirable features of a systems development environment are summarized in Table 2.1. As an example of illustration, the features supported by the structured methodologies are listed in the table (and highlighted by a check mark "√").

The structured models are not only familiar to practitioners in systems development, but have been found to be the most popular. They are taught in universities and polytechnics which offer courses in information systems analysis and design. They fully support users in making an abstract representation of the real world. More than one model can be used for different purposes or different stages in a typical development process. For example, the data flow school would use flowgraphs such as DeMarco data flow diagrams for analysis and use trees such as Yourdon structure charts ,for design, whereas the data structure school would use trees such as Jackson structure charts for initial analysis and use flowgraphs such as system specification diagrams to supplement the design. Specification details can also be expressed in a textual form like DeMarco's structured English or Jackson's structure texts. One distinct feature of all these models is that they support multiple levels of abstraction and refinement. Transformation processes are recommended to convert one model to another. The multi-model approach allows the initial analysis to be independent of the final implementation. Furthermore, because of the hierarchical structure of the models, modifications to a specification can be handled relatively easily.

However, the structured methodologies do not support a formalism for validating a specification. Nor do they support a mathematical framework whereby the transformation of one model to another is guaranteed. The main purpose of the unifying framework presented in this book is to provide a more comprehensive coverage of the systems development process. It supports a theoretical foundation guaranteeing that structured models can be mapped from one form to another. It also provides a mechanism for locating the unstructured components of a given data flow diagram or flowchart. On the practical side, an interactive graphical user-interface has been developed whereby data flow diagrams can be entered into the system and manipulated according to the needs of the users. Transformation to other models such as Yourdon structure charts and Jackson structure texts can also done through the system. The theoretical framework can be transparent to users who do not want to be involved with mathematical details. Features of the unifying framework are highlighted by the symbol "√*" in Table 2.1.

ABSTRACTION OF THE REAL WORLD	
User Familiarity of the Specification Language	√
Language Style	
• Textual language	√
• Graphical language	√
• Hybrid language	√
Multi-level Abstraction	√
Feedback to Users	
• Interactive graphics input	√*
• Generation of documentation and graphics	√*
• Prototyping	×
Modifiability	√

LEGEND:	√	Supported by structured models
	√*	Supported by unifying framework
	×	Not supported

**Table 2.1 Features of Unifying Framework for Structured Models
(Part 1 of 2)**

MANIPULATION OF REPRESENTATIONS	
Tools for Manipulation	
• Formalism	√*
• Mathematical rigour	√*
Transformation	
• Support of different development situations	√
• Transparency of formalism	√*
Validation	
• Syntactic consistency	√*
• Continuity	√*
• User verification	√*
Independence of Design and Implementation	√
CONSTRUCTION OF REAL SYSTEM	
Computability	
• File design and optimization	×
• Process design and optimization	×
Verification of Implementation	
• Traceability	×
• Proof of correctness	×

Table 2.1 Features of Unifying Framework for Structured Models
(Part 2 of 2)

3 A Comparison with Related Work

3.1 INTRODUCTION

In this chapter we shall compare our approach with five related systems development environments. These environments include PSL/PSA, ADS/SODA, SADT/EDDA, SAMM/SIGS and RSL/SREM. They have been chosen for comparison because of the following reasons:

(a) They were pioneer systems development environments meant to cover the entire systems life cycle, and have stood the test of time.

(b) They are better known and documented, so that interested readers can obtain further information easily.

(c) They are still under active development and recent enhancements have been reported.

(d) The languages examined cover a wide spectrum of characteristics. Some were originally developed as manual tools, but others were meant for mechanical support from the very beginning. For some languages, a system can be specified in a multi-level fashion, but not for others. Some languages use graphics as the specification medium while others are purely textual. Some of the development environments generate graphical feedback to users whereas others generate textual documentation.

(e) The final reason is a pragmatic one. We have included projects which are familiar to the present author. Part of this chapter is derived from the research results of a joint project with Mr Daniel Pong (Tse and Pong 1982, Tse and Pong (to appear)).

3.2 PSL/PSA AND META/GA

PSL was the first major language for defining a system formally and analysing it automatically (Teichroew 1971, Teichroew *et al.* 1980, 1982, *PSL/PSA Introduction* 1987). It was developed by the ISDOS project at the University of Michigan and is now a commercial product marketed by ISDOS Inc. The system consists of a Problem Statement Language (PSL), a Problem Statement Analyser (PSA) and a database for maintaining information on the target system, as shown in Figure 3.1.

PSL is a relational, non-procedural, machine-processable language. Its syntax is formally defined. The statements cover system structure, system input/output flows, data structures, data derivations, system properties, system behaviour and project

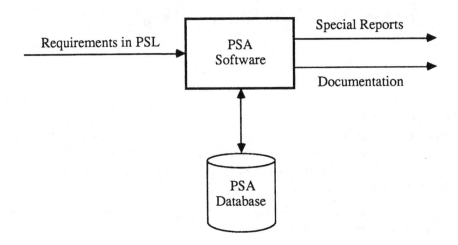

Figure 3.1 An Overview of PSL/PSA

management. The underlying principle is the entity-relationship-attribute (ERA) model (Chen 1976). (This appears, however, to be an afterthought since the ERA approach was not available when PSL/PSA was first introduced.) Thus PSL statements are formal descriptions of entities, attributes, and binary relationships between entities. Descriptive comments in natural English can also be included to enhance readability.

The Problem Statement Analyser is a collection of programs developed for analysing and processing PSL statements and maintaining them in a database. Lexical, syntactic and semantic analyses performed by PSA include the following: data definition analysis; volume analysis; static analysis, which checks the syntactic consistency of the input statements; and dynamic analysis, which determines the behavioural properties of the processes. Documentation and reports can be produced interactively.

Although PSL can only be input as a textual language and hence is one-dimensional in nature, a set of graphical reports can be generated automatically for the convenience of user verification. Unfortunately, users must go back to the source PSL statements for modification. Furthermore, there is no facility to help users to correlate the graphical reports with source PSL statements.

PSL supports multi-level refinement, so that systems can be specified in a hierarchical manner. The specifications are independent of design and implementation, and are traceable against the target systems. Information is centralized through the database. Syntactic consistency checks can be made automatically by the machine. Statements can be modified without causing major changes to the rest of a specification. There are, however, quite a few drawbacks: There is no means to specify performance requirements and no means for obtaining an early view of the target system. Furthermore, PSL was not designed to fit into any systems development framework. When attempts were made to incorporate PSL/PSA into various development methodologies. such as SODA (see Section 3.4), it was found that enhancements of PSL were often necessary to suit particular frameworks.

The last drawback is particularly disturbing. The META/GA system is an attempt to solve the problem (Teichroew *et al.* 1980, Yamamoto 1981). An overview of the system is shown in Figure 3.2. Instead of using one common PSL for all applications, the formal description of a tailor-made PSL must be defined for a given development

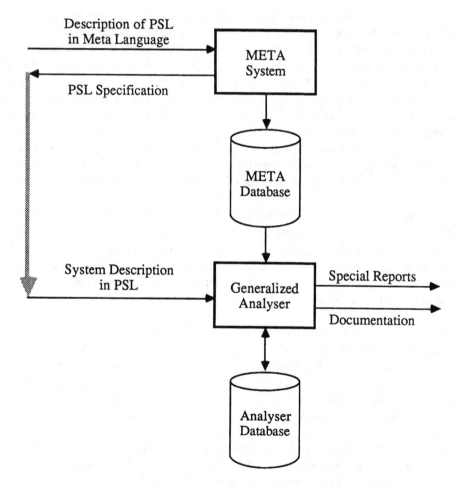

**Figure 3.2 Application of the META/GA System
to Generate a Specific PSL/PSA System**

methodology and input to the META system. An appropriate Generalized Analyser (GA) is then generated automatically. Systems descriptions can then be formulated using that particular PSL and manipulated by the GA in the same way that standard PSL is handled by PSA. This approach has been tested on the structured methodologies. According to the originator's own comments, "the results ... indicate that META/GA is a useful tool" (Yamamoto 1981).

3.3 ADS/SODA

Accurately Defined Systems (ADS) was an internal standard of NCR (*Study Guide* 1969) but was subsequently released for public use. It was originally meant to be a manual procedure.

Based on the notion that systems development should be results-oriented, an ADS systems description starts with the definition of all the systems output. It is then completed by the descriptions of systems input, computation, historical data retained in the system for a period of time, and the accompanying logic which is used to derive the output. A complete ADS systems description then consists of five types of interrelated forms, represented by the acronym *RICHL*. They include *R*eport definition forms, *I*nput definition forms, *C*omputation definition forms, *H*istory definition forms and *L*ogic definition forms. Each line of a form is uniquely identified by a 3-tuple: (Definition type, Page number, Line number). In this way, any piece of data on a report definition can be traced backwards to its originating source. For example, (I, 2, 3) would indicate that the data comes from page 2 line 3 of the Input definition.

ADS has been incorporated into the System Optimization and Design Algorithm (SODA) to form an integrated computer-aided methodology for the development of an financial management system (Nunamaker 1971, Nunamaker and Konsynski 1976). The methodology consists of ADS, SODA Statement Language (SSL), ADS analyser, SODA Statement Analyser (SSA), SODA Generator of Alternatives (SGA) and SODA Performance Evaluator (SPE).

SSL statements are used to provide design parameters and performance requirements not available in the ADS description. The ADS description and SSL statements are analysed and validated by the two analysers. A series of summary reports are produced. They consist of a data dictionary, indexes to all data elements and processes, incidence matrices of data elements required by each process, precedence matrices of data elements and processes, and graphical displays of the input ADS forms.

The output of the analyser and a statement of the available computing resources, hardware and utility programs are accepted by the SGA to analyse alternative hardware and software resources with respect to a specific design generated by the SGA. The output is a set of specifications of alternative designs stating the necessary CPU, memory size, program structure and data structure.

SPE helps in optimizing feasible designs to improve on the systems performance. It is made up of a series of mathematical programming models and timing routines. Its functions include optimization of the blocking factors for files, determining the number and type of auxiliary memory devices, allocation of files to memory devices and generation of an operations schedule.

The ADS/SODA integrated system deals with both the analysis and design phases of the systems development cycle. Systems specifications can be processed mechanically to ensure continuity and syntactic consistency. Transition into the design phase is straightforward. Optimization of files and program structures are performed by the SPE, but the optimization of program structures may cut across functional boundaries and may lead to maintenance problems.

The main drawback of ADS is that it is based entirely on the conventional systems development life cycle. ADS forms present too much detail to users, and complex systems cannot be represented in a hierarchical manner. No graphical representation is available for user-understanding. The designs generated are machine dependent, since a particular design is based on a particular choice of hardware. No formal framework is provided for checking the correctness of the design. It is doubtful whether the environment can be adapted to suit current systems development methodologies.

3.4 SADT/EDDA

Structured Analysis and Design Technique (SADT) was developed by SofTech Inc. (Dickover *et al.* 1978, Ross and Schoman 1977) based on the fundamental concepts of Ross (1977, 1980). It is essentially a structured decomposition discipline with a graphical means of expression, and can be applied to a wide range of systems.

The fundamental building block of an SADT specification is an activity, represented by a box linked at the four sides by arrows, as shown in Figure 3.3. The Input, Output and Control arrows specify the interfaces of this activity with other activities. The Mechanism arrow shows the support to accomplish the activity.

An SADT systems description consists of a hierarchy of inter-related networks of such activities. The top level SADT diagram shows the overall network structure of the target system. Each activity may be decomposed into a separate diagram with another network of boxes and arrows, as shown in Figure 3.4. The decomposition of activities can be continued at lower levels according to strict syntactical and semantic rules, so that a multi-level specification can be defined. A natural language or an artificial language for a particular application can be embedded into this graphical framework. The coupling of the two languages becomes the specification medium for that application. In this way, the embedded language cannot be used in an arbitrary fashion but must follow definite guidelines, hence reducing the effect of possible errors.

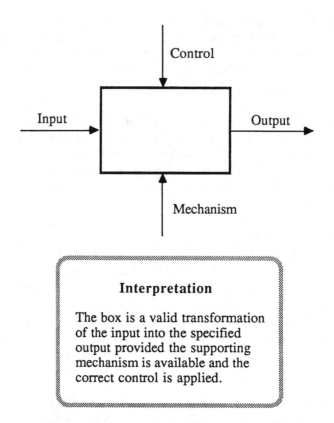

Figure 3.3 An SADT Fundamental Building Block

SADT provides a graphical means of refining a problem and expressing the solution. However, rules to analyse the continuity and syntactic consistency of the specification are not provided. Neither is there any means to express performance requirements. Although SADT provides systems analysts with a useful visual aid, the large number (about 40) of primitive constructs and concepts would cause difficulty in user-understanding (Colter 1984). As the complexity of a target system increases, it is fairly difficult to handle the technique manually. Moreover, the concept of Mechanism may mislead analysts to deal prematurely with implementation issues.

When SADT was originally designed, it was not meant to be mapped to an automatic supporting environment. The fundamental concept of "omitting the obvious", for instance, is only suitable for manual methodologies. EDDA is an attempt to incorporate mathematical formalism into SADT, so that the static and behavioural properties of a proposed system can be analysed (Trattnig and Kerner 1980). An extended Petri net (Peterson 1981, Reisig 1984) is used as the mathematical model for semantic definition. Transitions in Petri nets correspond to activities in SADT, and

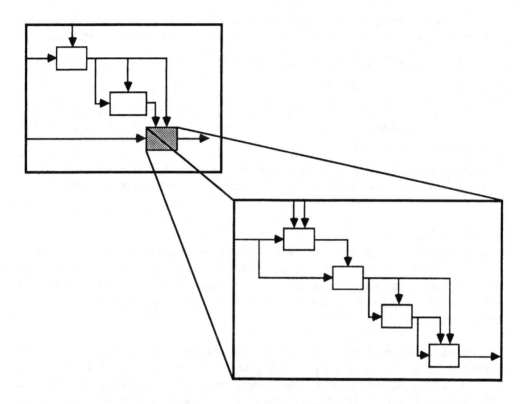

Figure 3.4 Decomposition of a Box in an SADT Diagram

places in Petri nets correspond to data items. To support the complex structure of SADT, EDDA extends the Petri net concept to include predicates and coloured tokens at transitions and places. Delay times and probabilities of activation are also included to facilitate the specification of performance requirements and the analysis of behavioural properties of target systems.

EDDA exists in two forms. The graphical form G-EDDA is identical to SADT and is for human understanding. The symbolic form S-EDDA is for computer processing. Since the two forms have corresponding syntaxes and identical semantics, one can easily be transformed into the other.

EDDA is an attempt to provide a formalism to an existing graphical language. It has all the positive characteristics of SADT. In addition, it has a textual representation which is in one-to-one correspondence with a graphical representation. The language is formal with a mathematical model transparent to users. Specifications are modifiable and traceable against the target systems, but like SADT, they are quite dependent on the process design of the final systems. EDDA is very similar to our present project in the sense that both are attempts to provide a formal basis to a structured graphical specification language. It has, however, four major drawbacks:

(*a*) It is restricted to SADT and cannot be linked to other structured methodologies.

(*b*) SADT is not the most popular of the structured models.

(*c*) Not every one of the 40 features of SADT has a Petri net counterpart. Even if such a correspondence exists, the large number of concepts and notations will hinder user-understanding.

(*d*) Even if a user is familiar with SADT, he must learn a new textual language S-EDDA because the latter is the only means of input to the development environment.

3.5 SAMM/SIGS

Systematic Activity Modelling Method (SAMM) was developed by the Boeing Computer Services Co. (Lamb *et al.* 1978, Peters and Tripp 1978, Stephens and Tripp 1978). It uses a language which is a combination of the prominent features of graphics with graph-theoretic notions, such that the resulting language can be machine-processed.

A specification consists of a context tree, activity diagrams and condition charts. The context tree, as shown the upper part of Figure 3.5, is effectively a table of contents for activity diagrams, expressed in a hierarchical form. An activity diagram, as shown in the lower part of Figure 3.5, is a network of rectangular boxes representing activities, and arrows representing data flows. Although similar to SADT diagram in appearance, these do not have the concepts of Controls or Mechanisms. The activity diagram also includes a data table, which consists of a narrative description specifying the data items involved, and a decomposition trace showing the respective data structures. Associated with each activity diagram is a condition chart, which describes the input and activity requirements for the production of output.

Each element of SAMM can be formulated mathematically. The mathematical models behind context trees and activity diagrams are labelled trees and directed graphs, respectively. A total systems description is thus a tree structure whose nodes are flowgraphs. In this way, the theory of trees and graphs can be applied to analyse a systems specification. The syntactic consistency of the specification, for instance, can be verified by checking whether each activity diagram is a connected graph and whether each output state is reachable from some input state through a finite number of paths.

Although SAMM has not been designed to fit any particular systems development methodology, an activity diagram can be regarded as a special type of data flow diagrams and can therefore be adapted to structured analysis. Unlike DeMarco data flow diagrams, however, it does not have the concept of file.

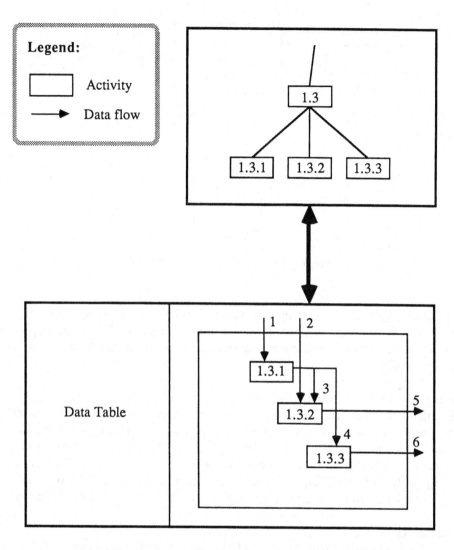

**Figure 3.5 Relationship between a Context Tree
and an Activity Diagram in SAMM**

An automated tool, SAMM Interactive Graphic System (SIGS), has been developed to implement SAMM. The functions of SIGS include model generation, model editing, model display, verification, report generation and model status control (see Figure 3.6). Various analyses can be performed on the SAMM model input to the SIGS. They include: syntax analysis to ensure that the input conforms to SAMM methodology, data flow analysis to verify the continuity of data passing from one diagram to another, decomposition analysis to ensure syntactic consistency between parent and child diagrams, and global analysis to highlight any redundant

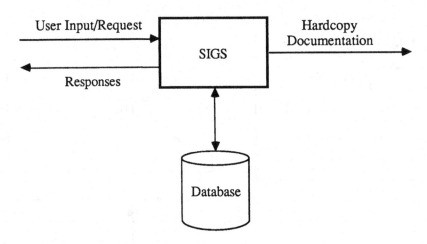

Figure 3.6   An Overview of SIGS

specification. Syntactic consistency is further verified by checking the connectivity and reachability of the graph structure in the activity diagram. Diagnostic reports and documentation of selected subsets of the model can be generated by using the report generation facility.

The language used in SAMM has many of the desirable features of a systems specification language, such as graphical representation, multi-level refinement and machine processability. The specifications are independent of design and implementation, can be modified easily, and is traceable against the target systems. Not much consideration, however, has been given to users who would like some form of textual input, especially for specifying the lowest level of a target system. Furthermore, the statics-only model cannot be used to specify or analyse performance requirements.

3.6 RSL/SREM

Software Requirements Engineering Methodology (SREM) was developed by TRW Defence and Space Systems Group (Alford 1977, 1980, 1982, 1985). The methodology consists of a Requirements Statement Language (RSL) and the Requirements Engineering and Validation System (REVS). An overview of SREM is shown in Figure 3.7.

The fundamental approach of SREM is to specify software requirements in terms of processing paths, each of which represents a sequence of operations connecting the arrival of an input message (or stimulus) to the generation of an output message (or response). Each operation is known as a processing step or simply an Alpha. The processing paths and steps are represented in a graphical form known as Requirements nets, or simply R-nets, as shown in Figure 3.8. In order to support stepwise

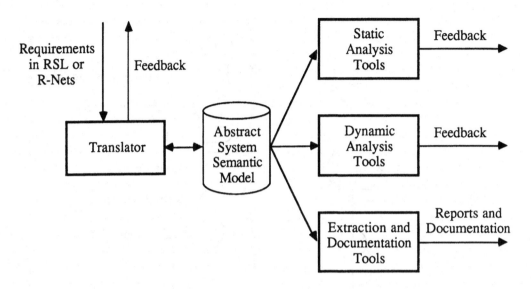

Figure 3.7 An Overview of SREM

refinement in systems development, the description of any Alpha in an R-net can be replaced by a number of lower level Alphas. Unlike structured DeMarco data flow diagrams or SADT, however, the authors of SREM prefer the final documentation to appear in only one layer rather than as a hierarchy of R-nets. Intermediate stages of decomposition will not be documented. Only a flat network will be shown in the final form.

RSL can also be represented in a textual form. The statements consists of four types of primitives: elements, binary relationships between elements, attributes of elements, and structures. The first three primitives deal with the non-procedural aspects of user requirements similarly in style to the entity-relationship-attribute approach. The structures are used to define the flow characteristics of the requirements. They are in fact the result of projecting R-nets on to a one-dimensional space. In this way, R-nets can be specified explicitly through an interactive graphical tool, or implicitly through the structure statements. While the structures are strictly defined in RSL to provide a rigid framework, the specifications of the other three primitives are more flexible and can be adapted to suit particular applications and future needs.

REVS consists of the RSL translator, the Abstract System Semantic Model (ASSM) and a set of analysis tools. The RSL translator is obtained through a compiler-writing system, so that any future change in RSL can be implemented easily. The ASSM is a relational database for maintaining information on software requirements. A flexible extraction package is available for generating documentation and special reports. Analysis tools have been developed to analyse the information stored in the ASSM.

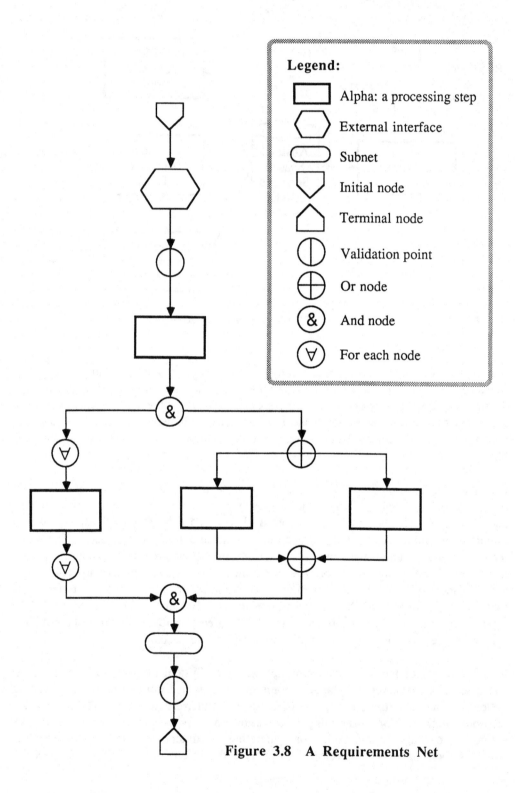

Figure 3.8   A Requirements Net

They include: static analysis tools which check the syntactic consistency of the R-net structure and the data flows, and dynamic analysis tools which generate simulators semi-automatically to check the behavioural properties of the target system. For example, performance requirements can be specified in the R-nets at various validation points. Such requirements can be verified dynamically against run-time statistics.

RSL has equivalent graphical and textual representations. The specifications are independent of design and implementation, modifiable, and traceable against the target systems. The mathematical formalism is transparent to users. It has been designed to fit into a complete systems development framework (Davis and Vick 1977) and is found to be a sophisticated and effective tool for the requirements definition and analysis of large systems (Scheffer and Rzepka 1984). Continuity and syntactic consistency checks of an RSL specification can be done automatically in SREM. Performance requirements are formally stated by the use of validation points. Semi-automatic simulation is provided in SREM for analysing the behavioural properties of the target system. This provides analysts and end users with a clear perception of the target system at an early stage. A process design engineering methodology has been reported, but the progress of development is not known. The major drawback of RSL is that, although it is said to support stepwise refinement, it is not reflected in the resulting documentation. The final specification in its flat form may not be understood by users who have not been involved with the development process. Furthermore, deficiencies have been reported on the friendliness of user-interface and on the performance of the analysis and simulation tools in SREM (Scheffer *et al.* 1985).

3.7 COMPARISON AND CONCLUSION
A summary of the features of five related systems development environments is shown in Table 3.1. Our current project of providing a unifying framework for the structured models is also listed side by side for comparison.

In most of the work examined, researchers have seen the need to propose a formal basis for information systems development. They have proposed the use of graphics in most cases (except ADS/SODA), to be supplemented by textual languages for defining details (except in the case of SAMM/SIGS). The need for providing a hierarchical framework in a specification is also recognized (except ADS/SODA and RSL). Feedback to users is provided either through interactive graphics (as in the case of SAMM/SIGS and RSL/SREM) or through graphics generated by the system (as in the case of PSL/PSA and SADT/EDDA). Validation of continuity and syntactic consistency are provided, except in the case of SADT/EDDA. File and process design is supported by most of the development environments, although optimization is not considered in most cases.

Since most of these environments started off with formal frameworks, they involve newly invented languages and result in a psychological distance between users and the development tools. Projects such as PSL/PSA have recognized the deficiency and have enhanced their systems to allow for interface with more popular tools such as the structured methodologies.

The main difference of our approach from the other projects lies in the fact that an existing set of popular specification languages, namely the structured systems development models, have been chosen as the starting point of the study. A mathematical framework is built on a set of interface languages which have proven popularity and success in systems development. The formalism remains transparent because users

	PSL/ PSA	ADS/ SODA	SADT/ EDDA	SAMM /SIGS	RSL/ SREM	Unifying Framewk
ABSTRACTION OF THE REAL WORLD						
User Familiarity of the Specification Language	×	×	√×	×	×	√
Language Style						
• Textual language	√	√	√	×	√	√
• Graphical language	√×	×	√	√	√	√
• Hybrid language	√	×	√	√×	√	√
Multi-level Abstraction	√	×	√	√	√×	√
Feedback to Users						
• Interactive graphics input	×	×	×	√	√	√
• Generation of documentation and graphics	√	×	√	√	√	√
• Prototyping	×	×	×	×	√×	×
Modifiability	√	×	√	√	√	√

LEGEND:	√	Supported
	√×	Partially supported
	×	Not supported

Table 3.1 A Comparison of the Features of Related Work
(Part 1 of 2)

	PSL/ PSA	ADS/ SODA	SADT/ EDDA	SAMM /SIGS	RSL/ SREM	Unifying Framewk
MANIPULATION OF REPRESENTATIONS						
Tools for Manipulation						
• Formalism	√	√×	√	√	√	√
• Mathematical rigour	×	√×	√	√	√	√
Transformation						
• Support of different development situations	√	√	√	√	√	√
• Transparency of formalism	×	×	√×	√	√	√
Validation						
• Syntactic consistency	√	√	×	√	√	√
• Continuity	√	√	√	√	√	√
• User verification	√	√	×	√	√	√
Independence of Design and Implementation	√	×	√×	√	√	√
CONSTRUCTION OF REAL SYSTEM						
Computability						
• File design and optimization	√×	√	√×	√×	√×	×
• Process design and optimization	√×	√	√×	√×	√×	×
Verification of Implementation						
• Traceability	√	×	√	√	√	×
• Proof of correctness	×	×	×	×	×	×

**Table 3.1 A Comparison of the Features of Related Work
(Part 2 of 2)**

communicate with the system through interactive graphics using DeMarco notation. Given the formal framework, mechanisms for validation as well as the aids to systems development can then be added to the system.

Only one other project discussed in this chapter employs an existing language as the start off point for creating a mathematical framework. Namely, SADT is chosen as the graphical language for EDDA.* Unfortunately, EDDA may be in fact be hindered by SADT, since the latter is not as popular as other structured models because of the extreme complexity of its graphical notation. Besides, EDDA accepts only textual input and generates graphics afterwards, and hence the formalism is not transparent to users.

---

* ADS/SODA is not considered to be in the same category since ADS is just a conventional form-based textual language without proven record of popularity or success.

4 An Initial Algebra Framework for Unifying the Structured Models

4.1 INTRODUCTION

Chapters 4 and 5 describe a unifying framework for the structured systems development models. Such a framework is useful for several reasons:

(a) Many projects to provide theoretical support for systems development do not use the popular structured analysis and design models. As pointed out in Davis (1982) and Martin (1983, 1984), practitioners are rather hesitant to use new tools that involve an unfamiliar formal language. On the other hand, a unifying theoretical framework that adds formal components to the notations of structured specifications permits users to continue using existing popular practices.

(b) Different structured models are suitable for different situations, depending on the characteristics of user requirements, the emphasis and the stage of development (Colter 1982, Lauber 1982, Sanden 1989, Shigo et al. 1980). In other words, we may need more than one of these tools during the development process of a single system. If we provide systems developers with a means of mapping from one model to another, the efficiency of systems development may be greatly improved.

(c) A number of development aids have been designed for individual structured models (Delisle et al. 1982, DeMarco and Soceneantu 1984, Kampen 1982, Tse 1985, Tse and Pong 1989). However, these aids are useful only for individual models, and are not applicable to others. If a mapping can be found to transform one model to another, a development aid for one structured methodology may be applied to another.

(d) In informal specifications such as DeMarco data flow diagrams, a certain degree of omission or "mutual understanding" is permitted. However, this often leads to ambiguity and misunderstanding. If a formal specification is used, we can enforce predefined standards more easily.

(e) Although information systems development, otherwise known as software engineering or information engineering, is claimed by many practitioners as an engineering discipline, most of the tools in practice are not supported by any theoretical framework. Unlike the more established engineering disciplines, it is not possible for a software engineer to determine whether a system has been developed according to user specifications and is completely free of errors (Parnas 1985). It is hoped that the unifying framework proposed in this book will provide a theoretical basis for the structured methodologies, and hence help to justify the classification of information systems development as an engineering discipline.

In this chapter, we propose to use an initial algebra framework for unifying the structured systems development models. Initial algebras have a rich mathematical theory (Burstall and Goguen 1982, Goguen *et al.* 1977). At the same time, the concepts can be simply stated for those who do not want to be involved with elaborate theories. We shall define the algebra and illustrate how it can be related to Yourdon structure charts (Figure 4.1), structured DeMarco data flow diagrams (Figure 4.2) and Jackson structure texts (Figure 4.3) by means of homomorphisms and equations. These three types of structured models have chosen for discussion because they have three distinct physical appearances, namely trees, flowgraphs and texts.

Only a knowledge of elementary set theory is assumed in this book. Readers who are interested in a deeper understanding of initial algebras may refer to Ehrig and Mahr (1985), Goguen *et al.* (1978), Meseguer and Goguen (1985) and Reichel (1987) for computer science oriented treatments, and to Goguen *et al.* (1975) and Wagner *et al.* (1977) for category-theoretic treatments.

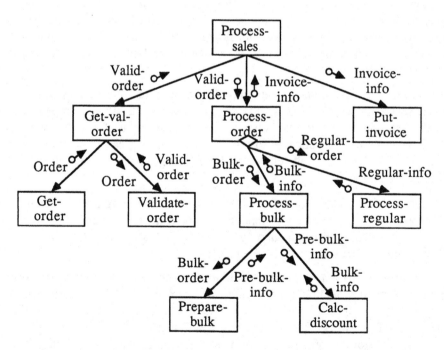

Figure 4.1 Sample Structure Chart in Yourdon Algebra

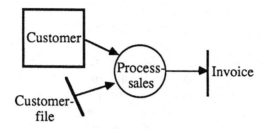

Process-sales:

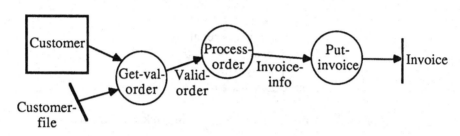

Get-val-order:

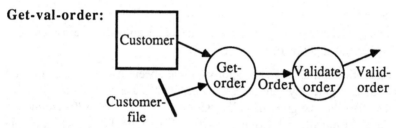

Process-order:

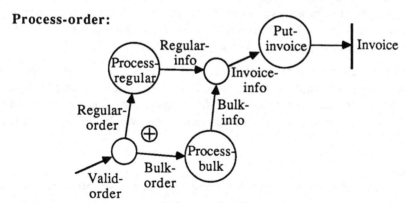

Process-bulk:

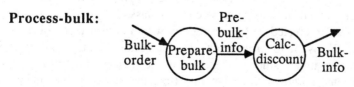

Figure 4.2   Sample Data Flow Diagram in DeMarco Algebra

```
process-sales seq
    get-valid-order seq
        get-order;
        validate-order;
    get-valid-order end;
    process-order sel
        process-bulk seq
            prepare-bulk;
            calc-discount;
        process-bulk end;
    process-order alt
        process-regular;
    process-order end;
    put-invoice;
process-sales end;
```

Figure 4.3   Sample Structure Text in Jackson Algebra

Besides the advantages of a unifying framework as stated above, there are some additional virtues of an initial algebra framework:

(*f*) In recent years the initial algebra approach has been used extensively in the specification of computer systems, making particular use of abstract data types. Examples are OBJ (Futatsugi *et al.* 1985, Goguen and Tardo 1979, Goguen *et al.* 1990) and Clear (Burstall and Goguen 1980, 1981, Sannella 1984). Interpreters for such languages are already available. Although such interpreters are not originally intended for structured analysis and design models, they can nevertheless be adapted to suit our needs, say, for validating our specifications.

(*g*) Because of the general nature of algebras, this approach does not assume any geometrical shape for entities to be modelled. Thus it can link structured DeMarco data flow diagrams which are flowgraphs, Yourdon structure charts which are tree structures, and Jackson structure texts which are in a sequential text format.

4.2   ALGEBRAS

In studying the properties of systems of a complex nature, we often classify the objects under consideration into different types. For example, we may have object types like booleans and integers in computer science, or tasks and events in information systems. We are also interested in the operations which act on these objects and generate other objects. We want to provide an abstract notion of these object types, independent of the objects under study. The formal mechanism for defining these object types and operations is known as a signature (like the key signature in music). More formally, a *signature* consists of a set S of object types, known as *sorts*, together with a family Σ of sets, each set containing *operation symbols* (or simply *symbols*) which relate the sorts. We shall use $\Sigma_{s_0 \dots s_n, s}$ to denote the set of operation symbols relating the sorts $s_0, \dots, s_n$ to the sort s.

Signatures would be of no use unless we could interpret them as the concrete objects which we wanted to study. This is achieved through the notion of algebras. An algebra A interprets the sorts and operation symbols as families of sets and functions. Each sort s is interpreted as a set A_s, which is called the *carrier* of A of sort s, and each symbol σ in $\Sigma_{s_0 \dots s_n, s}$ is mapped to a function

$$\sigma_A : A_{s_0} \times \dots \times A_{s_n} \to A_s$$

which is called an *operation* of A.

As an example, let us consider Boolean expressions. Various notations are commonly used by different people, such as:

(a)	**true**	**false**	**not**(t)	**and**(t, t')	**or**(t, t')
(b)	T	F	$\neg t$	$(t \wedge t')$	$(t \vee t')$
(c)	**true**	**false**	**not** t	$(t$ **and** $t')$	$(t$ **or** $t')$

We know that these classes of notations are in fact equivalent. There must be an abstract notion behind Boolean expressions, independent of any specific notation. We will define it using the above concept of a signature. Thus, the signature of Boolean expressions contains of one object type, which we will call the *boolean* sort. It also contains three classes of operation symbols. The symbol $\ominus$ relates a boolean to another boolean. The symbols $\otimes$ and $\oplus$ relates two booleans to a third boolean. The symbols ① and ⓪ are *constants*. In other words, they generate a boolean from nothing. The Boolean signature is defined more formally as follows:

$$\Sigma_{boolean\ boolean,\ boolean} = \{\otimes, \oplus\}$$
$$\Sigma_{boolean,\ boolean} = \{\ominus\}$$
$$\Sigma_{\Lambda,\ boolean} = \{①, ⓪\}$$

where Λ denotes an empty string.

The relationship among various sorts and operations can be represented graphically using an ADJ diagram, named after the ADJ Group (Joseph Goguen, James Thatcher, Eric Wagner and Jesse Wright) at IBM T.J. Watson Research Center, Yorktown Heights in 1972 (Goguen 1989). An ADJ diagram for the Boolean signature is shown in Figure 4.4.

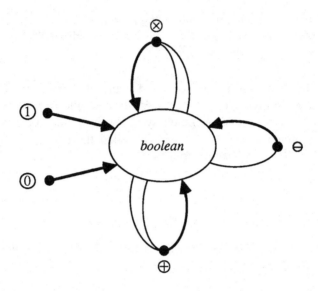

Figure 4.4 ADJ Diagram for the Signature *Boolean*

The sort can be mapped to a carrier $A_{boolean}$, which can be chosen to be a set of strings containing "**true**", "**false**", "**not**", "**and**" and "**or**". The symbols can be mapped to the following operations:

$$①_A : \to A_{boolean}$$
$$⓪_A : \to A_{boolean}$$
$$\ominus_A : A_{boolean} \to A_{boolean}$$
$$\otimes_A : A_{boolean} \times A_{boolean} \to A_{boolean}$$
$$\oplus_A : A_{boolean} \times A_{boolean} \to A_{boolean}$$

such that, for any t and t' in $A_{boolean}$,

$$①_A = \mathbf{true}$$
$$⓪_A = \mathbf{false}$$
$$\ominus_A(t) = \mathbf{not}\ t$$
$$\otimes_A(t, t') = \mathbf{and}(t, t')$$
$$\oplus_A(t, t') = \mathbf{or}(t, t')$$

In this way, Boolean expressions are seen as the result of operations on $A_{boolean}$.

The advantage of the algebraic concept lies in the fact that we map the same sort to another carrier $B_{boolean}$, which can be the set of strings containing "T", "F", "$\neg$", "$\wedge$" and "$\vee$". The operation symbols can then be mapped to another set of operations. Thus, for any t and t' in $B_{boolean}$, we have:

$$①_B = T$$
$$⓪_B = F$$
$$\ominus_B(t) = \neg t$$
$$\otimes_B(t, t') = (t \wedge t')$$
$$\oplus_B(t, t') = (t \vee t')$$

Let us now apply these algebraic fundamentals to structured systems. Conceptually, a structured system is specified by a hierarchy of *tasks*. Each task consists of the name of a main process, its underlying structure, together with the overall input and output which we shall call *events*. The structure determines whether the task is elementary, or is made up of subtasks in the form of sequence, selection, iteration or parallel connection. The input/output events are in the form of pure data related with other tasks, flags related with other tasks, files, or direct user input/output.

The signature for structured systems, then, consists of a set S of sorts:

   task, procname, struct, event, dataname

and a family Σ of sets of operation symbols:

$$\Sigma_{procname\ event\ event\ struct,\ task} = \{\textbf{task}\}$$
$$\Sigma_{\Lambda,\ procname} = \{\textbf{null}\} \cup P$$
$$\Sigma_{task\ task,\ struct} = \{\textbf{sequ, seln, para}\}$$
$$\Sigma_{task,\ struct} = \{\textbf{iter}\}$$
$$\Sigma_{\Lambda,\ struct} = \{\textbf{elem}\}$$
$$\Sigma_{dataname,\ event} = \{\textbf{indata, inflag, infile, source,}$$
$$\quad\quad\quad\quad\quad\quad\quad \textbf{outdata, outflag, outfile, sink}\}$$
$$\Sigma_{\Lambda,\ dataname} = E$$
$$\Sigma_{event\ event,\ event} = \{\_+\_\}$$
$$\Sigma_{\Lambda,\ event} = \{\textbf{nil}\}$$

where P is the set of all process names in a target system, and E is the set of all data names. The underscores (_) before and after the $+$ sign indicates that the latter is an infix operator. In other words, we write $e + e'$ instead of $+(e, e')$. An ADJ diagram for the signature for structured models is shown in Figure 4.5.

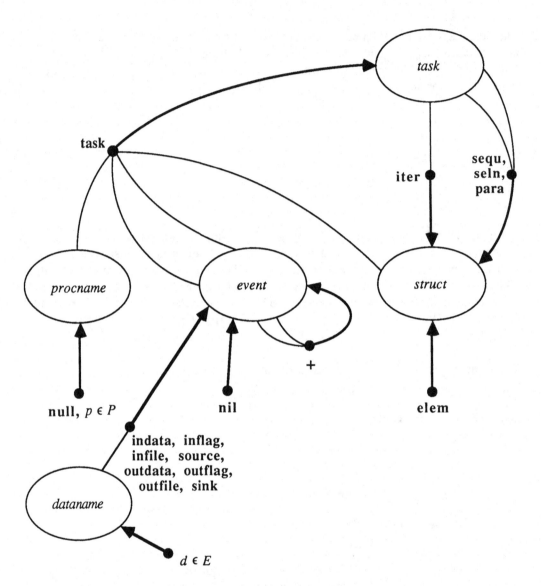

Figure 4.5 ADJ Diagram for the Signature for Structured Models

The sorts of the signature are mapped to the carriers as shown in Table 4.1. The symbols have the following interpretations:

(a) The operation **task**$_E$ links up the name of the main process in a task, the structure of its components, and its input/output events.

(b) The operations in P are constants specifying the names of the processes in the target system.

Sort	Carrier
task	set of tasks
procname	set of names of main processes in tasks
struct	set of structures
event	set of input/output events
dataname	set of names of data items

Table 4.1 Mapping of Sorts to Carriers in Structured Systems

(c) The operation **null**$_E$ indicates a process with no specific name.

(d) The operations **sequ**$_E$, **seln**$_E$, **iter**$_E$ and **para**$_E$ link up a number of subtasks to form a structure.

(e) The operation **elem**$_E$ indicates an elementary structure. In other words, it does not consist of subtasks.

(f) The operations **indata**$_E$, **inflag**$_E$, **infile**$_E$ and **source**$_E$ denote, respectively, input events consisting of pure data from another task, a flag from another task, data from a file, or direct input by users.

(g) The operations **outdata**$_E$, **outflag**$_E$, **outfile**$_E$ and **sink**$_E$ are similarly used for output events.

(h) The operations in E are constants specifying the data names in the input/output events.

(i) If an input event is made of more than one data item, they are linked up by the operation $+_E$. Similarly for an output event.

(j) The operation **nil**$_E$ indicates an input or output event with no actual data present.

In order to supply semantics or meaning to the operations, we also define *equations*, or relationships governing the behaviour of the operations. For example:

(i) Commutative law holds for the operations **seln** and **para**:

$$\textbf{seln}_E(u, v) = \textbf{seln}_E(v, u)$$
$$\textbf{para}_E(u, v) = \textbf{para}_E(v, u)$$

but it does not hold for the operation **sequ**.

(ii) Associative law holds for the operations **sequ**, **seln** and **para** when there is no intermediate process name:

$$\mathbf{sequ}_E(\mathbf{task}_E(\mathbf{null}_E, \mathbf{sequ}_E(u, v)), w)$$
$$= \mathbf{sequ}_E(u, \mathbf{task}_E(\mathbf{null}_E, \mathbf{sequ}_E(v, w)))$$

$$\mathbf{seln}_E(\mathbf{task}_E(\mathbf{null}_E, \mathbf{seln}_E(u, v)), w)$$
$$= \mathbf{seln}_E(u, \mathbf{task}_E(\mathbf{null}_E, \mathbf{seln}_E(v, w)))$$

$$\mathbf{para}_E(\mathbf{task}_E(\mathbf{null}_E, \mathbf{para}_E(u, v)), w)$$
$$= \mathbf{para}_E(u, \mathbf{task}_E(\mathbf{null}_E, \mathbf{para}_E(v, w)))$$

(*iii*) Furthermore, if we create an error supersort for every sort in our signature, and specify conditional equations, then more complex behavioural rules can also be defined. For instance, we can specify that, given a sequence of two tasks, an error message should be produced if the output event of the first task disagrees with the input event of the second. Thus:

$$\mathbf{sequ}_E(\mathbf{task}_E(p_0, e_0, e_1, s_0), \mathbf{task}_E(p_1, e_2, e_3, s_1)) = \mathbf{error}_E \text{ if } e_1 \neq e_2$$

4.3 INITIAL ALGEBRAS

As shown above, different algebras can be defined over the same signature. *Homomorphisms*, which are families of functions that preserve the operations, can be defined from one algebra to another. They allow us to express relationships between algebras, including subalgebra, quotient algebra and equivalent algebra relationships. In particular, isomorphisms, or homomorphisms which map between two equivalent algebras, can help us to express change of representation. Such homomorphisms enable us to forget about minor syntactical differences in various representations and concentrate on the main issues.

More formally, we define a homomorphism $h: A \rightarrow B$ as a family of functions $(h_s: A_s \rightarrow B_s)_{s \in S}$ satisfying two conditions:

(*H1*) For any symbol σ in $\Sigma_{\Lambda, s}$, $h_s(\sigma_A) = \sigma_B$.

(*H2*) For any operation symbol σ in $\Sigma_{s_0 \dots s_n, s}$, and for any elements $x_0, \dots, x_n$ in A_{s_0}, $\dots, A_{s_n}$, respectively, $h_s(\sigma_A(x_0, \dots, x_n)) = \sigma_B(h_{s_0}(x_0), \dots, h_{s_n}(x_n))$. †

For example, consider an algebra F, which we shall call a shilly-shally algebra. The carrier is a set of strings containing "**perhaps**", "**true**", "**false**", "**not**", "**and**" and "**or**". The operation symbols are mapped as follows:

---

† In order to avoid clumsy layers of subscripts, we shall simply use $h(x)$ to denote $h_s(x)$ or $h_{s_i}(x)$ whenever the sort s or s_i is self-evident from the context. The equation in (*H2*), for instance, can be written as $h(\sigma_A(x_0, \dots, x_n)) = \sigma_B(h(x_0), \dots, h(x_n))$.

$$①_F = \textbf{true}$$
$$⓪_F = \textbf{false}$$
$$⊖_F(t) = \textbf{not } t$$
$$⊗_F(t, t') = \textbf{and}(t, t')$$
$$⊕_F(t, t') = \textbf{or}(t, t')$$

A unique homomorphism can be defined from A to F by simply mapping strings in A to the same strings in F. On the other hand, more than one homomorphism can be defined in the reversed direction. The main reason is that F contains a junk word **"perhaps"** which is not related to the original signature. We can, for instance, define a function f which maps strings in F to strings in A by substituting each occurrence of the word **"perhaps"** in a string by the word **"true"**. In this way,

> **and(perhaps, or(true, false))**

in F will be mapped to

> **and(true, or(true, false))**

in A. We can also define a second function g which maps strings in F to strings in A by substituting each occurrence of the word **"perhaps"** in a string by the word **"false"**. Thus,

> **and(perhaps, or(true, false))**

in F will be mapped to

> **and(false, or(true, false))**

in A. Both f and g are homomorphisms because all the strings involving symbols in the original signature will remain unchanged, and hence definitions ($H1$) and ($H2$) for homomorphisms will be satisfied.

Consider another example G, which we shall call a wishful algebra. The carrier is a set containing only the word **"true"**. We let

$$①_G = \textbf{true}$$
$$⓪_G = \textbf{true}$$
$$⊖_G(t) = \textbf{true}$$
$$⊗_G(t, t') = \textbf{true}$$
$$⊕_G(t, t') = \textbf{true}$$

A function $h: A \to G$ mapping every string in A to **"true"** in G will obviously satisfy the definitions ($H1$) and ($H2$) for homomorphisms. However, a reversed homomorphism $k: G \to A$ does not exist because the operations $①_G$ and $⓪_G$ have been confused or mixed up in the algebra G. We would otherwise have contradictions like

$$\textbf{false} = \ominus_A(\textcircled{1}_G) = k(\ominus_G(\textcircled{1}_G)) = k(\textcircled{1}_G) = \textbf{true}$$

It turns out that the algebra A we have defined is the best algebra for the Boolean signature. It contains *no junk* (quite unlike the shilly-shally algebra) and *no confusion* (quite unlike the wishful algebra). It is called an *initial algebra*, and exhibits the following property:

> An algebra A is initial if and only if, for any algebra B over the same signature, there exists a unique homomorphism mapping A to B.

In order for the concept of initial algebra to be useful in practice, we must be able to prove its existence by actually constructing one such algebra for any given signature. This can be done through the idea of a term algebra. The algebra A in the Boolean example above is in fact a term algebra.

We shall apply this concept to structured models. We shall construct a *term algebra* T_Σ for structured systems, and prove that it is initial.

(A) *Carriers:* Let us enlarge the set Σ of symbols by putting in three "delimiter" symbols: "(", ";" and ")". The carriers of T_Σ are made up of *terms* in Σ, or strings of symbols from Σ. We define the carriers $(T_\Sigma)_s$ by induction as follows:

(A1) For any symbol σ in $\Sigma_{\Lambda, s}$, let the term "σ" be in $(T_\Sigma)_s$.

(A2) For any operation symbol σ in $\Sigma_{s_0 \ldots s_n, s}$, and for any terms $t_0, \ldots, t_n$ in $(T_\Sigma)_{s_0}, \ldots, (T_\Sigma)_{s_n}$, respectively, let the term "$\sigma(t_0; \ldots; t_n)$" be in $(T_\Sigma)_s$.

(B) *Operations:* Operations σ_T in T_Σ are induced from the symbols σ as follows:

(B1) For any symbol σ in $\Sigma_{\Lambda, s}$, we define σ_T to be the term "σ".

(B2) For any operation symbol σ in $\Sigma_{s_0 \ldots s_n, s}$, and for any terms $t_0, \ldots, t_n$ in $(T_\Sigma)_{s_0}, \ldots, (T_\Sigma)_{s_n}$, respectively, we define $\sigma_T(t_0, \ldots, t_n)$ to be the term "$\sigma(t_0; \ldots; t_n)$".

We shall prove in the remaining part of this section that the term algebra T_Σ thus defined is an initial algebra. In other words, it can be mapped by unique homomorphisms to other algebras over the same signature. To do this, we shall construct an algebra X, prove that it is the same as T_Σ, and that it is initial. Furthermore, we shall illustrate in the next sections how the terms in T_Σ, such as the example shown in Figure 4.6, can be related to Yourdon structure charts, structured DeMarco data flow diagrams and Jackson structure texts such as the examples in Figures 4.1 to 4.3.

Let i_A and i_B be the identity functions on the algebras A and B, respectively. That is to say, for any x in A and y in B, $i_A(x) = x$ and $i_B(y) = y$. Suppose $h: A \rightarrow B$ and

$k: B \to C$ are two homomorphisms. Let $k \circ h: A \to C$ denote the composite function. In other words, for any x in A, $k \circ h(x) = k(h(x))$. A homomorphism $h: A \to B$ is defined as an *isomorphism* if and only if there exists a homomorphism $k: B \to A$ such that $k \circ h = i_A$ and $h \circ k = i_B$. In this case we write $k = h^{-1}$. Two algebras A and B over the same signature are said to be *isomorphic* to each other if and only if there exists an isomorphism $h: A \to B$.

Proposition 4.3.1

Let A be an initial algebra over the signature Σ. If B is another algebra over the same signature, then B is initial if and only if A is isomorphic to B.

Proof: Suppose A is isomorphic to B. Then there is a homomorphism $h: B \to A$. Let C be any algebra over the same signature Σ. Since A is initial, there is a unique homomorphism $k: A \to C$. Hence there exists a homomorphism $k \circ h: B \to C$. We need only prove that the homomorphism is unique. Indeed, for any homomorphism $l: B \to C$, the mapping $l \circ h^{-1}$ is a homomorphism from A to C. By the uniqueness of k, we must have $k = l \circ h^{-1}$. So $k \circ h = l \circ h^{-1} \circ h = l$, and hence B is initial.

Conversely, suppose B is initial. Then there exist unique homomorphisms $h: A \to B$ and $k: B \to A$. Since A is initial and both $k \circ h$ and i_A are homomorphisms mapping A to A, we must have $k \circ h = i_A$. Similarly, since B is initial and both $h \circ k$ and i_B are homomorphisms mapping B to B, we must have $h \circ k = i_B$. Hence h is an isomorphism or, in order words, A is isomorphic to B. $\square$

task (process-sales; **source** (customer) + **infile** (customer-file); **outfile** (invoice);
sequ (**task** (get-valid-order; **source** (customer) + **infile** (customer-file); **outdata** (valid-
            order);
        sequ (**task** (get-order; **source** (customer) + **infile** (customer-file); **outdata** (order);
                elem);
            task (validate-order; **indata** (order); **outdata** (valid-order); **elem**)));
        task (**null**; **indata** (valid-order); **outfile** (invoice);
        sequ (**task** (process-order; **indata** (valid-order); **outdata** (invoice-info);
            seln (**task** (process-bulk; **indata** (bulk-order); **outdata** (bulk-info);
                sequ (**task** (prepare-bulk; **indata** (bulk-order); **outdata** (pre-bulk-info);
                    elem);
                    task (calc-discount; **indata** (pre-bulk-info); **outdata** (bulk-info);
                    elem)));
                task (process-regular; **indata** (regular-order); **outdata** (regular-info);
                elem)));
            task (put-invoice; **indata** (invoice-info); **outfile** (invoice); **elem**)))))

Figure 4.6 Sample Term in Initial Algebra

We shall construct X as a union of $X^{(j)}$ for all integers $j \geq 0$. We construct $X^{(j)}$ by mathematical induction as follows:

(a) For any sort s in S, we define $X_s^{(0)}$ as the set containing all terms of the form "σ", where each σ is a symbol in $\Sigma_{\Lambda, s}$. We define $X^{(0)}$ to be the family of all $X_s^{(0)}$.

(b) Suppose $X^{(i)}$ has been defined for all integers $i = 0, ..., j-1$. We define $X_s^{(j)}$ as the set containing all terms of the form "$\sigma(t_0; ...; t_n)$", where σ is a symbol in $\Sigma_{s_0 \ldots s_n, s}$ and each t_r is a term in $X_{s_r}^{(i_r)}$ such that $max\{i_r\} = j-1$. We define $X^{(j)}$ to be the family of all $X_s^{(j)}$.

To give X an algebraic structure, we define operations on X as follows:

(i) For any symbol σ in $\Sigma_{\Lambda, s}$, we define σ_X to be the term "σ" in $X_s^{(0)}$.

(ii) For any operation symbol σ in $\Sigma_{s_0 \ldots s_n, s}$, and for any terms $t_0, ..., t_n$ in $X_{s_0}^{(i_0)}$, ..., $X_{s_n}^{(i_n)}$, respectively, we define $\sigma_X(t_0, ..., t_n)$ to be the term "$\sigma(t_0; ...; t_n)$" in $X_s^{(j)}$, where $j = max\{i_0, ..., i_n\} + 1$.

Lemma 4.3.2
The algebra X is identical to the term algebra T_Σ.

Proof: First of all, we shall show $X \subseteq T_\Sigma$ by mathematical induction on $X^{(j)}$.

(a) Any term in $X_s^{(0)}$ is of the form "σ", where σ is a symbol in $\Sigma_{\Lambda, s}$. By definition, it must be in $(T_\Sigma)_s$. Hence $X^{(0)} \subseteq T_\Sigma$.

(b) Suppose $X^{(i)} \subseteq T_\Sigma$ for all integers $i = 0, ..., j-1$. Consider an arbitrary term in $X_s^{(j)}$. It must be of the form "$\sigma(t_0; ...; t_n)$" for some symbol σ in $\Sigma_{s_0 \ldots s_n, s}$ and terms t_r in $X_{s_r}^{(i_r)}$, where each i_r is an integer such that $max\{i_r\} = j-1$. Since each t_r is in $(T_\Sigma)_{s_r}$, the term "$\sigma(t_0; ...; t_n)$" must be in $(T_\Sigma)_s$. Hence $X^{(j)} \subseteq T_\Sigma$.

Conversely, we must prove $T_\Sigma \subseteq X$. Since T_Σ is defined by (A1) and (A2), we shall show that any term constructed through (A1) and (A2) must be in X.

(i) Suppose a term in $(T_\Sigma)_s$ is of the form "σ", where σ is a symbol in $\Sigma_{\Lambda, s}$. By definition, it must be in $X_s^{(0)}$ and hence in X.

(ii) Suppose a term in $(T_\Sigma)_s$ is of the form "$\sigma(t_0; ...; t_n)$", where σ is a symbol in $\Sigma_{s_0 \ldots s_n, s}$ and each t_r is a term in $X_{s_r}^{(i_r)}$. Let $j = max\{i_r\} + 1$. Then "$\sigma(t_0; ...; t_n)$" must be in $X_s^{(j)}$ and hence in X. $\square$

Lemma 4.3.3
The algebra X is initial over the signature Σ.

Proof: Let A be any algebra over the signature Σ. We need to prove that there exists a unique homomorphism h mapping X to A.

($h1$) We define $h: X^{(0)} \to A$ by setting $h(\sigma) = \sigma_A$ for any symbol σ in $\Sigma_{\Lambda, s}$.

($h2$) Suppose $h: X^{(i)} \to A$ has been defined for all integers $i = 0, ..., j-1$. Consider an arbitrary term t in $X^{(j)}$. It must be of the form "$\sigma(t_0; ...; t_n)$" for some symbol σ in $\Sigma_{s_0 ... s_n, s}$ and terms t_r in $X_{s_r}^{(i_r)}$, where each i_r is an integer such that $max\{i_r\} = j-1$. We define $h: X^{(j)} \to A$ by setting $h(t) = \sigma_A(h(t_0), ..., h(t_n))$.

Obviously h is a homomorphism. Let k be any homomorphism from X to A. By definition, it has the following two properties:

($k1$) For any symbol σ in $\Sigma_{\Lambda, s}$, $k(\sigma_X) = \sigma_A$.

($k2$) For any operation symbol σ in $\Sigma_{s_0 ... s_n, s}$, and for any terms $t_0, ..., t_n$ in $X_{s_0}, ..., X_{s_n}$, respectively, $k(\sigma_X(t_0, ..., t_n)) = \sigma_A(k(t_0), ..., k(t_n))$

We note that ($k1$) is equivalent to ($h1$) because σ_X in ($k1$) is in fact the term "σ" in ($h1$). Furthermore, ($k2$) is equivalent to ($h2$) because $\sigma_X(t_0, ..., t_n)$ in ($k2$) is in fact the term t in ($h2$). Hence any homomorphism $k: X \to A$ satisfies ($h1$) and ($h2$). In other words, there exists a unique homomorphism h mapping X to A. $\square$

We can therefore arrive at the main theorem on the proposed term algebra.

Theorem 4.3.4
The term algebra T_Σ is an initial algebra over Σ.

4.4 YOURDON STRUCTURE CHARTS

To illustrate how the terms in our initial algebra can be mapped to structure charts, we must first of all define an algebra Y of Yourdon structure charts (which we shall call *Yourdon algebra* for short). The signature for Yourdon algebra is the signature for structured systems defined in Section 4.2. The carriers are defined in Figure 4.7. The operations σ_Y are defined as shown in Figure 4.8. (An example is given in Figure 4.9 illustrating how the graphical notations should be interpreted.) Then the unique homomorphism will map our initial algebra to Yourdon algebra. The term in Figure 4.6, for example, will be mapped to the structure chart of Figure 4.1. In this way, a transformation system can be developed to provide a computerized link between the initial algebra and Yourdon algebra. It can accept any term in our initial algebra as input and generate a Yourdon structure chart automatically.

Can we do the reverse? That is to say, can we define a unique reversed homomorphism from Yourdon algebra to the initial algebra, and hence get back our term? The answer, unfortunately, is no. It is because quite a few operations are distinct in the term algebra but overlap in Yourdon algebra. For example, all of the operations **infile**$_Y$, **outfile**$_Y$, **source**$_Y$ and **sink**$_Y$ map any data name d into **nil**$_Y$. Another example is that both **sequ**$_Y$ and **para**$_Y$ give identical results. Yourdon algebra must therefore be extended to solve the "confusion" problem before a unique reversed homomorphism can be defined. The algebra of *extended* Yourdon structure charts can then be regarded as isomorphic to our term algebra.

(a) All the process names in $\Sigma_{\Lambda, procname}$ are in $Y_{procname}$.

(b) All the data names in $\Sigma_{\Lambda, dataname}$ are in $Y_{dataname}$.

(c) For any d in $Y_{dataname}$,

are in Y_{event}. Intuitively, this means that for any given data name d, events may be defined as an input data item (denoted by a white circle with a downward arrow), output data item (white circle with an upward arrow), input flag (black circle with a downward arrow) or output flag (white circle with an upward arrow) carrying that data name. The dotted enclosures are used only as "meta-parenthesis" in the definitions and are not part of Yourdon's notation. Further illustration on our graphical convention may be found in Figure 4.9.

(d) For any e and e' in Y_{event},

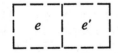

is in Y_{event}. This means that two events placed side by side will form another event.

Figure 4.7 Carriers of Yourdon Algebra
(Part 1 of 2)

(e) For any p in $Y_{procname}$, s in Y_{struct}, and e_i and e_o in Y_{event},

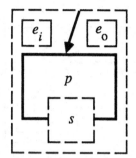

is in Y_{task}. Intuitively, this means that a task may be defined by putting together a process name p, a structure s and input/output events e_i and e_o.

(f) For any u and v in Y_{task},

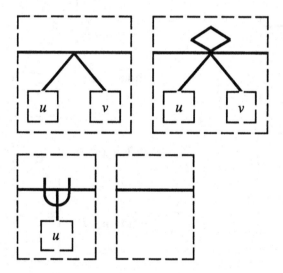

are in Y_{struct}. This means that structures may be defined as the sequence or selection of subtasks u and v, the iteration of a subtask u, or simply an elementary structure with no subtasks.

Figure 4.7 Carriers of Yourdon Algebra
(Part 2 of 2)

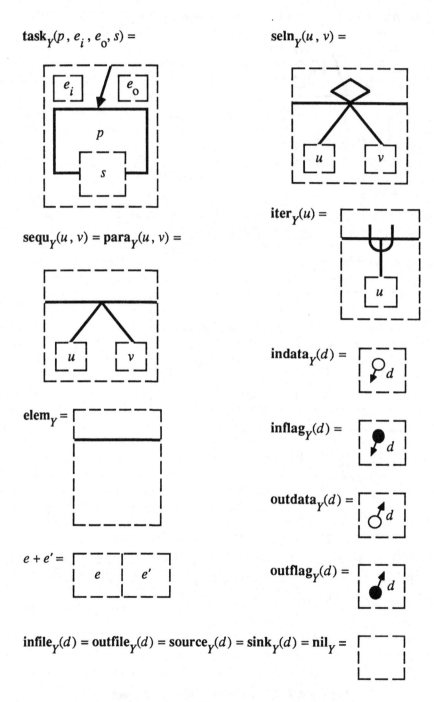

Figure 4.8 Operations in Yourdon Algebra

If we substitute

$$s = \mathbf{seln}_Y(u, v) =$$

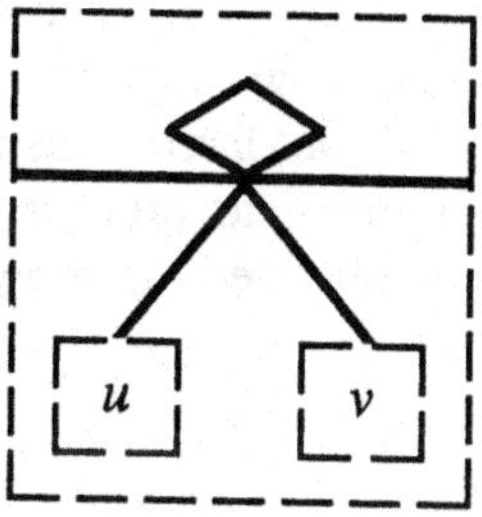

into

$$w = \mathbf{task}_Y(p, e_i, e_o, s) =$$

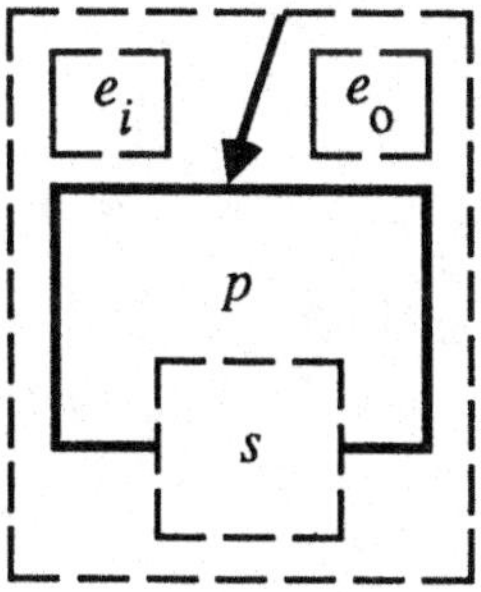

we get

$$w = \mathbf{task}_Y(p, e_i, e_o, \mathbf{seln}_Y(u, v)) =$$

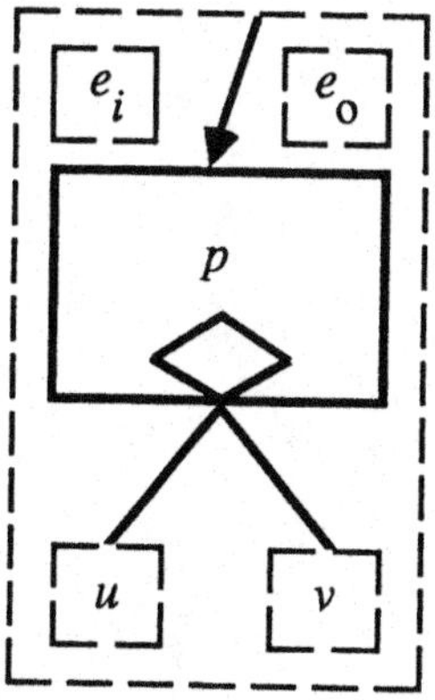

Figure 4.9 Example of Interpretation of
Graphical Operations in Yourdon Algebra

4.5 DeMARCO DATA FLOW DIAGRAMS

We can similarly define an algebra D of structured DeMarco data flow diagrams (or *DeMarco algebra* for short). The carriers are defined in Figure 4.10, and the operations are as shown in Figure 4.11. An example is given in Figure 4.12 illustrating how the graphical notations should be interpreted. The unique homomorphism will map the terms in our initial algebra to data flow diagrams. The term in Figure 4.6, for instance, can be mapped to the structured DeMarco data flow diagram of Figure 4.2. Furthermore, if we forget about the intermediate process names in the original term, then a flattened data flow diagram can be obtained, as shown in Figure 4.13.

(a) All the process names in $\Sigma_{\Lambda,\ procname}$ are in $D_{procname}$.

(b) All the data names in $\Sigma_{\Lambda,\ dataname}$ are in $D_{dataname}$.

(c) For any d in $D_{dataname}$,

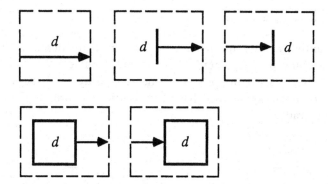

are in D_{event}. Intuitively, this means that for any given data name d, events may be defined as an data flow (denoted by a single arrow), input file (a thick bar followed by an arrow), output file (an arrow leading to a thick bar), data source (a box followed by an arrow) or data sink (an arrow leading to a box) carrying that data name. The dotted enclosures are used only as "meta-parenthesis" in the definitions and are not part of DeMarco's notation. Further illustration on our graphical convention may be found in Figure 4.12.

(d) For any e and e' in D_{event},

is in D_{event}. This means that two events placed side by side will form another event.

Figure 4.10 Carriers of DeMarco Algebra
(Part 1 of 2)

(e) For any p in $D_{procname}$, s in D_{struct}, and e_i and e_o in D_{event},

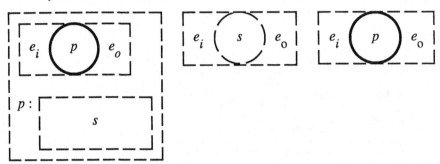

are in D_{task}. Intuitively, this means that a task may be defined by putting together a process name p, a structure s and input/output events e_i and e_o, as shown on the first diagram. If the process name is missing or if the structure is elementary (with no subtasks), we will have a simplified picture, as shown in the second and third diagrams.

(f) For any u and v in D_{task},

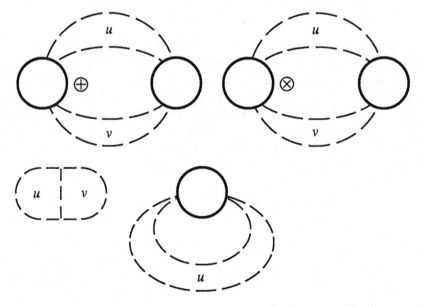

are in D_{struct}. This means that structures may be defined as the selection, parallel connection, or sequence of subtasks u and v, or the iteration of a subtask u.

Figure 4.10 Carriers of DeMarco Algebra
(Part 2 of 2)

$\text{task}_D(p, e_i, e_o, s) =$

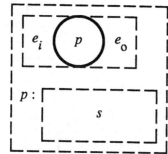

$\text{iter}_D(u) =$

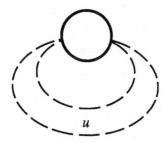

$\text{seln}_D(u, v) =$

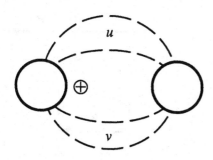

$\text{sequ}_D(u, v) =$

$e + e' =$

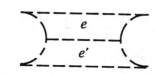

$\text{para}_D(u, v) =$

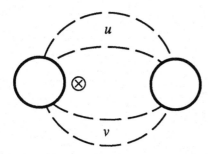

**Figure 4.11 Operations in DeMarco Algebra
(Part 1 of 2)**

$\text{indata}_D(d) = \text{inflag}_D(d) =$

$\text{outdata}_D(d) = \text{outflag}_D(d) =$

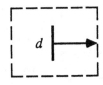

$\text{infile}_D(d) =$

$\text{outfile}_D(d) =$

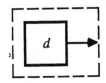

$\text{source}_D(d) =$

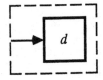

$\text{sink}_D(d) =$

subject to the following:

(a) $\text{task}_D(\text{null}_D, e_i, e_o, s) =$

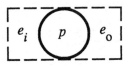

(b) $\text{task}_D(p, e_i, e_o, \text{elem}_D) =$

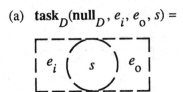

(c)

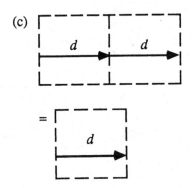

Figure 4.11 Operations in DeMarco Algebra
(Part 2 of 2)

If we substitute

$$u = \mathbf{task}_D(p_0, e_0, e_1, \mathbf{elem}_D) =$$

and

$$v = \mathbf{task}_D(p_0, e_2, e_3, \mathbf{elem}_D) =$$

into

$$s = \mathbf{seln}_D(u, v) =$$

we get

$$s = \mathbf{seln}_D(\mathbf{task}_D(p_0, e_0, e_1, \mathbf{elem}_D), \mathbf{task}_D(p_0, e_2, e_3, \mathbf{elem}_D)) =$$

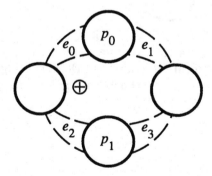

**Figure 4.12 Example of Interpretation of
Graphical Operations in DeMarco Algebra
(Part 1 of 2)**

Furthermore, if we substitute

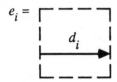

$$e_i =$$

into s, we get

$$s =$$

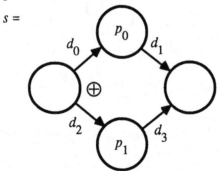

Figure 4.12 Example of Interpretation of
Graphical Operations in DeMarco Algebra
(Part 2 of 2)

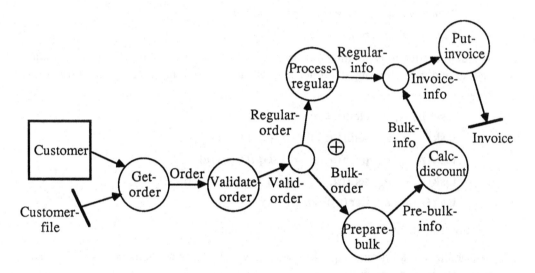

Figure 4.13 Flat Data Flow Diagram in DeMarco Algebra

4.6 JACKSON STRUCTURE TEXTS

We also want to define an algebra J of Jackson structure texts (or *Jackson algebra* for short). This is done by means of an algebraic concept of equations, and involves the following steps:

(*a*) We define a preliminary Jackson algebra which has the same carrier and operations as our term algebra.

(*b*) We define the signature for Jackson algebra by extending the original signature for structured models to include four new operation symbols:

$$\Sigma_{procname,\,task} = \{\,\_;\,\}$$
$$\Sigma_{procname\,task\,task\,procname,\,task} = \{\,\_seq\_\,\_\,\_end;\,\}$$
$$\Sigma_{procname\,task\,procname\,task\,procname,\,task} = \{\,\_sel\_\,\_alt\_\,\_end;\,\}$$
$$\Sigma_{procname\,task\,procname,\,task} = \{\,\_itr\_\,\_end;\,\}$$

(*c*) We define equations to link up the new operations with the original operations, and to indicate that input/output events are ignored in Jackson structure texts, thus:

$$\textbf{task}(p,\,e_i,\,e_o,\,\textbf{elem}) = p;$$
$$\textbf{task}(p,\,e_i,\,e_o,\,\textbf{sequ}(u,\,v)) = p\ \textbf{seq}\ u\ v\ p\ \textbf{end};$$
$$\textbf{task}(p,\,e_i,\,e_o,\,\textbf{para}(u,\,v)) = p\ \textbf{seq}\ u\ v\ p\ \textbf{end};$$
$$\textbf{task}(p,\,e_i,\,e_o,\,\textbf{seln}(u,\,v)) = p\ \textbf{sel}\ u\ p\ \textbf{alt}\ v\ p\ \textbf{end};$$
$$\textbf{task}(p,\,e_i,\,e_o,\,\textbf{iter}(u)) = p\ \textbf{itr}\ u\ p\ \textbf{end};$$

for any tasks u, v, events e_i, e_o and process name p.

(*d*) We define an additional equation so that we can forget about tasks whose main processes have no names:

$$\textbf{null seq}\ u\ v\ \textbf{null end};\ =\ u\ v$$

for any tasks u and v.

In this way, the unique homomorphism will enable us to map our terms into Jackson structure texts. This has been implemented using UMIST OBJ (Gallimore *et al.* 1989), which validates a given term and converts it into Jackson structure text. In this way, the term in Figure 4.6 will be validated and mapped to the structure text of Figure 4.3 using the OBJ program in Figure 4.14. The conversion process is known as *term rewriting*. If the left hand side of an equation appears in a given term, it will automatically be substituted by the corresponding right hand side. This will be done recursively until no more substitution is possible. Details of the term rewriting process for our example is shown in Figure 4.15.

```
obj procnames
sorts procname
ops
    calcDiscount: -> procname
    getOrder: -> procname
    getValidOrder: -> procname
    prepareBulk: -> procname
    processBulk: -> procname
    processOrder: -> procname
    processRegular: -> procname
    processSales: -> procname
    putInvoice: -> procname
    validateOrder: -> procname
    null: -> procname
jbo

obj datanames
sorts dataname
ops
    bulkInfo: -> dataname
    bulkOrder: -> dataname
    customer: -> dataname
    customer-file: -> dataname
    invoice: -> dataname
    invoiceInfo: -> dataname
    order: -> dataname
    preBulkInfo: -> dataname
    regularInfo: -> dataname
    regularOrder: -> dataname
    validOrder: -> dataname
jbo

obj events/datanames
sorts event
ops
     _+_ : event event -> event
    indata: dataname -> event
    inflag: dataname -> event
    infile: dataname -> event
```

**Figure 4.14 Applying UMIST OBJ to Term Algebra and Jackson Algebra
(Part 1 of 2)**

```
        source: dataname -> event
        outdata: dataname -> event
        outflag: dataname -> event
        outfile: dataname -> event
        sink: dataname -> event
        nil: -> event
jbo

obj tasks/procnames events
sorts atask struct
ops
        task: procname event event struct -> atask
        sequ: atask atask -> struct
        seln: atask atask -> struct
        para: atask atask -> struct
        iter: atask -> struct
        elem: -> struct
jbo

obj jackson/tasks
ops
        _; : procname -> atask
        _seq_ _ _end; : procname atask atask procname -> atask
        _sel_ _alt_ _end; : procname atask procname atask procname -> atask
        _itr_ _end; : procname atask procname -> atask
        _ _ : atask atask -> atask
vars
        u, v: atask
        p: procname
        eI, eO: event
        s: struct
eqns
        (task(p, eI, eO, elem) = p ;)
        (task(p, eI, eO, sequ(u, v)) = p seq u v p end;)
        (task(p, eI, eO, para(u, v)) = p seq u v p end;)
        (task(p, eI, eO, seln(u, v)) = p sel u p alt v p end;)
        (task(p, eI, eO, iter(u)) = p itr u p end;)
        (null seq u v null end; = u v)
jbo
```

Figure 4.14 Applying UMIST OBJ to Term Algebra and Jackson Algebra
(Part 2 of 2)

(a) *Original term:*

> **task**(process-sales, **source**(customer) + **infile**(customer-file), **outfile**(invoice),
> **sequ**(**task**(get-valid-order, **source**(customer) + **infile**(customer-file),
>   **outdata**(valid-order),
>   **sequ**(**task**(get-order, **source**(customer) + **infile**(customer-file),
>   **outdata**(order), **elem**),
>   **task**(validate-order, **indata**(order), **outdata**(valid-order), **elem**))),
>   **task**(**null**, **indata**(valid-order), **outfile**(invoice),
>   **sequ**(**task**(process-order, **indata**(valid-order), **outdata**(invoice-info),
>   **seln**(**task**(process-bulk, **indata**(bulk-order), **outdata**(bulk-info),
>   **sequ**(**task**(prepare-bulk, **indata**(bulk-order), **outdata**(pre-bulk-
>   info), **elem**),
>   **task**(calc-discount, **indata**(pre-bulk-info), **outdata**(bulk-
>   info), **elem**))),
>   **task**(process-regular, **indata**(regular-order), **outdata**(regular-
>   info), **elem**))),
>   **task**(put-invoice, **indata**(invoice-info), **outfile**(invoice), **elem**)))))

(b) *Step 1:*

> **task**(process-sales, **source**(customer) + **infile**(customer-file), **outfile**(invoice),
> **sequ**(**task**(get-valid-order, **source**(customer) + **infile**(customer-file),
>   **outdata**(valid-order),
>   **sequ**(get-order; ,
>   validate-order;)),
>   **task**(**null**, **indata**(valid-order), **outfile**(invoice),
>   **sequ**(**task**(process-order, **indata**(valid-order), **outdata**(invoice-info),
>   **seln**(**task**(process-bulk, **indata**(bulk-order), **outdata**(bulk-info),
>   **sequ**(prepare-bulk; ,
>   calc-discount;)),
>   process-regular;)),
>   put-invoice;))))

Figure 4.15 Example of Term Rewriting
(Part 1 of 3)

(c) *Step 2:*

> **task** (process-sales, **source** (customer) + **infile** (customer-file), **outfile** (invoice),
> **sequ** (get-valid-order **seq**
> > > get-order;
> > > validate-order;
> > get-valid-order **end**;,
> > **task** (**null**, **indata** (valid-order), **outfile** (invoice),
> > **sequ** (**task** (process-order, **indata** (valid-order), **outdata** (invoice-info),
> > > **seln** (process-bulk **seq**
> > > > prepare-bulk;
> > > > calc-discount;
> > > process-bulk **end**;,
> > > process-regular;)),
> > put-invoice;))))

(d) *Step 3:*

> **task** (process-sales, **source** (customer) + **infile** (customer-file), **outfile** (invoice),
> **sequ** (get-valid-order **seq**
> > > get-order;
> > > validate-order;
> > get-valid-order **end**;,
> > **task** (**null**, **indata** (valid-order), **outfile** (invoice),
> > **sequ** (process-order **sel**
> > > > process-bulk **seq**
> > > > > prepare-bulk;
> > > > > calc-discount;
> > > > process-bulk **end**;
> > > process-order **alt**
> > > > process-regular;
> > > process-order **end**;,
> > put-invoice;))))

(e) This is continued until the Jackson structure text of Figure 4.3 is produced.

Figure 4.15 Example of Term Rewriting
(Part 2 of 3)

Note: The bold face and indentation are shown above for the purpose of presentation only. They are not part of the input/output of the OBJ program in Figure 4.14. On the other hand, such syntactic sugar can easily be generated in the Jackson structure text if we include LaTeX commands in the OBJ code. For example, the last module of the OBJ program may be modified to read:

```
obj jackson/tasks
ops
    _; : procname -> atask

    _{\bf seq}\begin{quote}_\\_\end{quote}
    _{\bf end}; : procname atask atask procname -> atask

    _{\bf sel}\begin{quote}_\end{quote}
    _{\bf alt}\begin{quote}_\end{quote}
    _{\bf end}; : procname atask procname atask procname -> atask

    _{\bf itr}\begin{quote}_\end{quote}
    _{\bf end}; : procname atask procname -> atask

    _\\_ : atask atask -> atask

vars
    u, v: atask
    p : procname
    eI, eO: event
    s: struct

eqns
    (task(p, eI, eO, elem) = p ;)
    (task(p, eI, eO, sequ(u, v))
        = p {\bf seq}\begin{quote} u \\ v \end{quote} p {\bf end};)
    (task(p, eI, eO, para(u, v))
        = p {\bf seq}\begin{quote} u \\ v \end{quote} p {\bf end};)
    (task(p, eI, eO, seln(u, v))
        = p {\bf sel}\begin{quote} u \end{quote}
            p {\bf alt}\begin{quote} v \end{quote} p {\bf end};)
    (task(p, eI, eO, iter(u))
        = p {\bf itr}\begin{quote} u \end{quote} p {\bf end};)
    (null {\bf seq}\begin{quote} u \\ v \end{quote} null {\bf end};
        = u \\ v)
jbo
```

Figure 4.15 Example of Term Rewriting
(Part 3 of 3)

4.7 CONCLUSION

Structured analysis and design models can be integrated algebraically. A term algebra has been defined and can be mapped through homomorphisms to Yourdon structure charts, structured DeMarco data flow diagrams, and Jackson structure texts (with equations). As a result, specifications can be transformed from one form to another, as summarized in Figure 4.16. Algebraic interpreters may be adapted to validate the specifications. Automatic development aids for one methodology may be applied to another. On the other hand, the mathematical concepts can be made transparent to systems designers who do not want to be involved with complex theories.

One slight drawback of the algebraic framework is that, although the term algebra provides us with a model having no junk and no confusion, users may not be willing to specify systems in such a formal way. Even if we propose an extended Yourdon structure chart (which is isomorphic to the term algebra) as syntactic sugar, it is still against the standard practice in structured methodologies, where developers find DeMarco data flow diagrams more suitable in the early analysis phase, and would like only to convert them into structure charts later on in the design stage. The latter order of events is not available in the framework suggested in this chapter. In the next chapter, we shall look at the possibility of supporting such a reversed path of events through a category-theoretic framework.

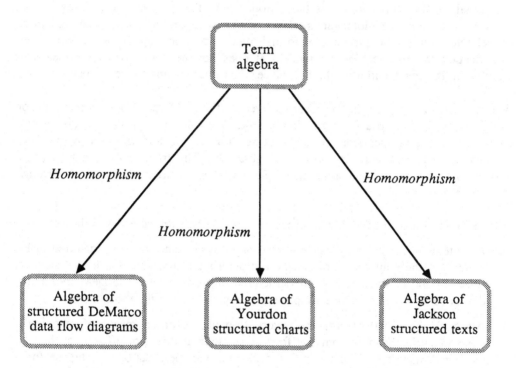

Figure 4.16 Linking the Structured Models by Term Algebra

5 A Functorial Framework for Unifying the Structured Models

5.1 INTRODUCTION

An initial algebra framework has been proposed in the last chapter to integrate the structured systems development models. Given a specification in one structured model, the framework provides a formal means of mapping it to an equivalent specification in terms of another model. It does not, however, provide a means of developing the specification in the first place. Not does it consider refinement.

We find that the proposed term algebra as well as the DeMarco, Yourdon and Jackson notations fit nicely into a functorial framework. We can integrate the models by providing functorial bridges from one type of specification to another. An overview of the functorial relationships is shown in Figure 5.1. The framework also provides a theoretical basis for manipulating incomplete or unstructured specifications through refinement morphisms.

The main advantages of the functorial framework can be summarized as follows:

(a) A systems developer may conceive the target system in terms of structured tasks, which are the equivalents of standard structuring mechanisms such as sequence, selection and iteration used in the structured methodologies. The DeMarco, Yourdon or Jackson notations are simply seen as variations on the same theme.

(b) Although the initial algebra framework provides a formal means of mapping a structured specification from one form to another, it does not offer much help at the initial stage when we are trying to develop the specification. Using the functorial framework, we can refine a draft specification of structured tasks using morphisms, which preserves structuredness. Properties of continuous functions and structured functions can be used to verify the correctness of such manipulation. These concepts help a systems developer to visualize the internal structure of a system, assemble or refine subsystems, and verify the consistency and completeness of a design.

(c) Using the properties of morphisms in structured tasks, the systems analyst can partially specify a system and refine it to whatever detail he sees fit at a later stage of development. Unlike defining a term in the initial algebra framework, there is no need for him to wait for a complete specification.

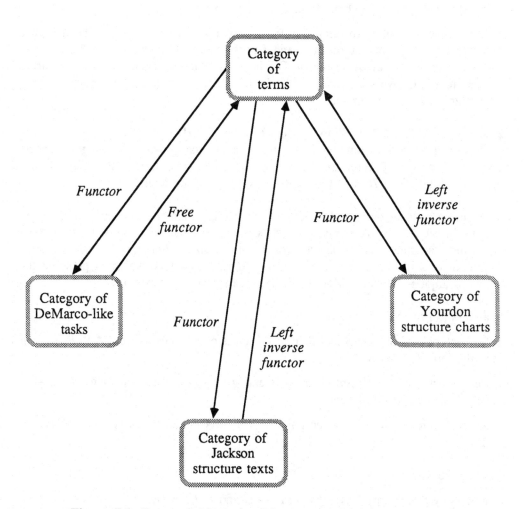

Figure 5.1 Functorial Relationships among Structured Models

(*d*) A system can only be specified as an algebraic term in the initial algebra framework if the system is structured. On the other hand, any system, structured or otherwise, can be specified as a task in the functorial framework. By means of the graph-theoretic properties of such a task, we can determine whether the system is in fact structured (see Chapter 6). A structured task can then be transformed into an algebraic term if the user so wishes.

(*e*) The conversion of a specification from one model to another can be achieved through the concepts of functors and free functors. For example, a functor can map terms in the initial algebra to DeMarco-like task diagrams or Yourdon structure charts. Conversely, terms in the initial algebra can be generated freely from DeMarco-like task diagrams.

5.2 A BRIEF INTRODUCTION TO CATEGORY THEORY

This section gives a brief introduction to the fundamental concepts in category theory. Interested readers may refer to Arbib and Manes (1975), Barr and Wells (1990), Goguen *et al.* (1973, 1976) and Goldblatt (1984) for further details.

The concepts of categories and functors are stronger than the concepts of sets and functions in set theory. A *category* consists of a collection of *objects*, together with relationships amongst these objects called *morphisms*. *Functors* can be defined mapping objects in one category to those of another category, so as to preserve the morphisms amongst objects. More formally, a category X consists of:

(*a*) a class $|X|$ of objects

(*b*) for each pair of objects A and B in $|X|$, a class of morphisms from A to B, written in the form $f: A \rightarrow B$

(*c*) for each pair of morphisms $f: A \rightarrow B$ and $g: B \rightarrow C$, a morphism $g \circ f: A \rightarrow C$ called the *composite* of f and g

(*d*) for each object A of $|X|$, a morphism $i_A: A \rightarrow A$ called the *identity morphism* at A,

subject to the following conditions:

(*i*)   given any morphisms $f: A \rightarrow B$, $g: B \rightarrow C$ and $h: C \rightarrow D$,

$$h \circ (g \circ f) = (h \circ g) \circ f$$

(*ii*) given any morphism $f: A \rightarrow B$,

$$f \circ i_A = i_B \circ f = f$$

Mappings between categories preserving the morphisms are called functors. More formally, a *functor* $F: X \rightarrow Y$ from a category X to another category Y consists of:

(*a*) a mapping of objects A in $|X|$ to objects $F(A)$ in $|Y|$

(*b*) a mapping of morphisms $f: A \to B$ in X to morphisms $F(f): F(A) \to F(B)$ in Y,

such that the composites and identity morphisms are preserved, that is to say,

(*i*) if $h = g \circ f$, then $F(h) = F(g) \circ F(f)$

(*ii*) $F(i_A) = i_{F(A)}$

As an illustration, let us define a category of strings, denoted by *String*. An object in $|String|$ is a set A^* of strings of elements from sets A, together with a concatenation operation $\bullet: A^* \times A^* \to A^*$ and an empty string Λ, such that

$$t \bullet (u \bullet v) = (t \bullet u) \bullet v$$
$$t \bullet \Lambda = \Lambda \bullet t = t$$

for any strings t, u and v in A^*. The morphisms in *String* are functions $f: A^* \to B^*$ which preserve the concatenation operation. That is to say, $f(t \bullet u) = f(t) \bullet f(u)$ for any strings t and u in A^*. We can easily verify that the conditions for composites and identities apply to such morphisms.

Similarly, we can define a category of sets, denoted by *Set*. Its objects are sets and its morphisms are functions. Furthermore, we can define a "forgetful" functor from *String* to *Set*. We map any set of strings A^* in $|String|$ to the underlying set A in $|Set|$. The morphisms in *String* are mapped to simpler morphisms in *Set* by forgetting about the concatenation operation and the empty string.

Conversely, given the forgetful functor $G: String \to Set$, there is a *left adjoint* or *free functor* $F: Set \to String$ which maps each set A to a set A^* of strings freely generated by A. This concept of a free functor will be very useful for structured models, as illustrated Section 5.6.

5.3 CATEGORY OF DeMARCO-LIKE PROCESSES
We construct a category of processes, to be denoted by *Process*. They can be represented graphically using DeMarco-like data flow diagrams, and hence the name "DeMarco-like processes". This category is a stepping stone to the category of DeMarco-like tasks shown in Figure 5.1.

5.3.1 Objects
The objects of *Process* are sets of processes. The concept of a process will be formally defined in this section. We shall also define the concept of a structured task, so that we can study, in the next section, morphisms which preserve structuredness. In this way, the usual notions of abstraction and refinement in structured methodologies can be formalized in a functorial framework.

Let P be a given set of process names such as "process-sales" and let D be a given set of data items such as "**source** customer" or "**file** customer-file". Let $E = D*$ be the set of events. In other words, each event e_j in E is of the form $<d_{j0}, ..., d_{jn}>$, where $d_{j0}, ..., d_{jn}$ are data items in D. We define a *standard process* to be an ordered triple $<e_0, p, e_1>$ for some process name p in P and events e_0 and e_1 in E. We call e_0 its *input* event and e_1 its *output* event, and we assume that $e_0 \neq e_1$. The following is a typical example:

<<**source** customer, **file** customer-file>, process-sales, <**file** invoice>>

For simplicity, when an event consists of only one data item, we shall omit the unnecessary angle braces, thus:

<<**source** customer, **file** customer-file>, process-sales, **file** invoice>

A standard process can also be represented diagrammatically, as shown in Figure 5.2(a).

Besides standard processes, we also need to define three *auxiliary processes* that have more than one input or output event each:

(a) A *decision* has one input event e_0 and two output events e_1 and e_2. It is denoted by $<e_0, \oplus, <e_1, e_2>>$.

(b) A *fork* has one input event e_0 and two output events e_1 and e_2 also. It is denoted by $<e_0, \otimes, <e_1, e_2>>$.

(c) A *join* has two input events e_0 and e_1 and one output event e_2. It is denoted by $<<e_0, e_1>, \bigcirc, e_2>$.

These processes can be represented diagrammatically as shown in Figure 5.2.

We define a *task* to be set of processes. In structured methodologies, we are interested in a particular class of tasks known as *structured tasks*. Conceptually, they are sets of processes linked up by four operations: sequence, selection, iteration and parallel connection. Although a structured task may be made up of a number of individual processes, it must have only one overall input event e_0 and only one overall output event e_1 ($\neq e_0$). Thus we can denote a structured task by $U(e_0, e_1)$. It is defined recursively as follows:

(i) An *elementary task* $U(e_0, e_1)$, which consists of one and only one standard process $<e_0, p, e_1>$, is a structured task.

(ii) The *sequence* of any two structured tasks $U_0(e_0, e_1)$ and $U_1(e_1, e_2)$, defined as

$$(U_0 \bullet U_1)(e_0, e_2) = U_0(e_0, e_1) \cup U_1(e_1, e_2)$$

is a structured task.

(a) **Standard Process:**

(b) **Decision:**

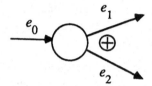

(c) **Fork:**

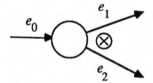

(d) **Join:**

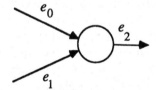

Figure 5.2 Diagrammatic Representation of Processes

(*iii*) The *selection* of any two structured tasks $U_0(e_0, e_1)$ and $U_1(e_2, e_3)$, defined as

$$(U_0 \oplus U_1)(e_4, e_5) = \{<e_4, \oplus, <e_0, e_2>>\} \cup U_0(e_0, e_1) \cup U_1(e_2, e_3)$$
$$\cup \{<<e_1, e_3>, \bigcirc, e_5>\}$$

is a structured task.

(*iv*) The *parallel connection* of any two structured tasks $U_0(e_0, e_1)$ and $U_1(e_2, e_3)$, defined as

$$(U_0 \otimes U_1)(e_4, e_5) = \{<e_4, \otimes, <e_0, e_2>>\} \cup U_0(e_0, e_1) \cup U_1(e_2, e_3)$$
$$\cup \{<<e_1, e_3>, \bigcirc, e_5>\}$$

is a structured task.

(v) The *iteration* of any structured task $U(e_0, e_1)$, defined as

$$*(U)(e_2, e_3) = \{<<e_2, e_1>, \bigcirc, e_4>\} \cup U(e_0, e_1)$$
$$\cup \{<e_4, \oplus, <e_0, e_3>>\}$$

is a structured task.

To ease user-understanding, we can represent structured tasks by DeMarco-like task diagrams, as shown in Figure 5.3. We note that they differ from standard DeMarco data flow diagrams in two aspects:

(a) In a task diagram, all the input events for a bubble are lumped together as one arrow, but this is not the case for standard data flow diagrams. This applies also to output events.

(b) Standard data flow diagrams may not necessarily be structured.

The reason is that DeMarco data flow diagrams are mainly used during the analysis stage of systems development. They are used to document the real life situation, which may not be structured (in the sense of sequence, selection, iteration and parallel connection). However, as recommended by most authors on structured design, we would like to convert them into other representations such as Yourdon structure charts. In this case, we would regard such data flow diagrams as control flowgraphs, and would like them to be structured. As we shall see later on in this chapter, DeMarco-like task diagrams are extremely useful for this purpose.

It is quite easy to convert standard data flow diagrams into task diagrams if the latter can be unstructured. We need only lump the input and output events together, as shown in Figure 5.4. It would, however, be more complex if we want to convert them into structured task diagrams. In the next chapter, we are going to look at the method of detecting unstructuredness in an arbitrary flowgraph, so that it can be converted into a structured flowgraph. As a result, standard data flow diagrams can always be converted into structured task diagrams, so that the functorial framework defined in this chapter can be applied.

5.3.2 Morphisms

In our first attempt to define morphisms in the category of DeMarco-like processes, we tried to look as structured tasks as open sets and apply continuous functions similar in style to general net theory (Fernandez 1975, 1976 and Genrich *et al.* 1980). It was found, however, that openness and continuous functions did not serve our needs because they were too general. The morphisms more appropriate to the category of processes are structured functions, as defined in Section (*b*) below. Nevertheless, continuous functions will still be discussed briefly in Section (*a*) because they include structured functions as a special case, and help us to link our theory with the more

(a) **Elementary Task:**

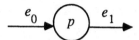

(b) **Sequence:**

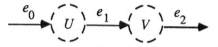

(c) **Selection:**

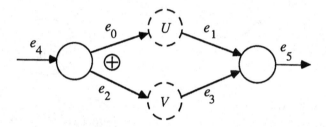

(d) **Parallelism:**

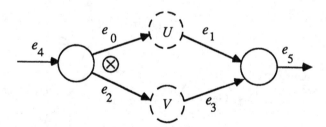

(e) **Iteration:**

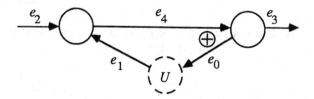

Figure 5.3 Diagrammatic Representation of Structured Tasks

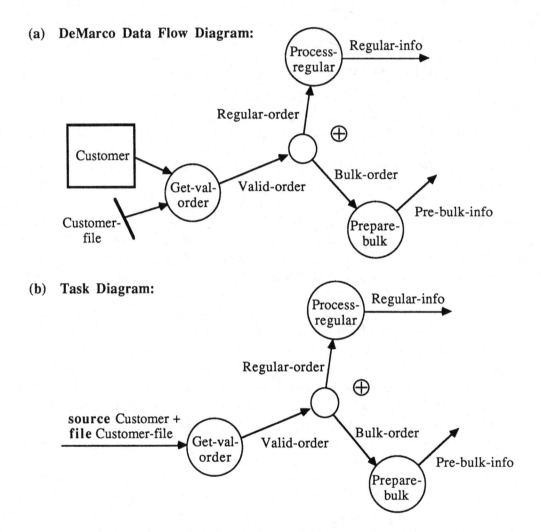

**Figure 5.4 Comparison between DeMarco Data Flow Diagrams
and Task Diagrams**

general results of net topology.

(a) *Continuous functions:* Given a structured task T, a subtask $U \subseteq T$ is said to be *open* if and only it is a finite union of structured tasks (possibly none). On the other hand, a task containing, for example, only auxiliary processes will not be open. The set of all open tasks in T thus defined forms a topology, since it has the following properties:

> T is open,
> $\varnothing$ is open,
> the unions of finite number of open tasks are open,
> the intersections of open tasks are open.

Continuous functions $f: T \to T'$ can be defined in the usual manner. That is to say, f is continuous if and only if, for any open task $V \subseteq T'$, $f^{-1}[V]$ is also an open task $\subseteq T$. It can be shown (Fernandez 1975) that the set of processes together with continuous functions form a category.

We find, however, that it is not too useful for us to employ continuous functions as morphisms in our category of structured tasks. This is due to two reasons:

(i) Although any structured task must be open, not every open task is structured. For example, let e_0 and e_1 be distinct events. The task

$$U = \{ <e_0, p_0, e_1>, <e_1, p_1, e_0> \}$$

is open because it is the union of two elementary (and hence structured) tasks. However, the combined task is a self-loop and is therefore unstructured.

(ii) Not all continuous functions preserve the structuredness of the tasks that they handle. For instance, U in the example above may be mapped by a continuous function to an elementary task

$$V = \{ <e_0, p_0, e_1> \}$$

Even though openness is preserved, we would not like such functions to appear in structured methodologies, because we are mapping an unstructured self-loop U to a structured task V, or in other words, allowing a structured task V to be refined into an unstructured self-loop U.

(b) *Structured functions:* We would like to define another class of functions which preserve structuredness. Formally, a function $f: T \to T'$ is said to be *structured* if and only if, for any structured task $V \subseteq T'$, $f^{-1}[V]$ is structured.

The concept of structured functions is very useful in the structured methodologies because structuredness will be preserved when we map one task to another. But how are structured functions actually constructed? This is achieved through the concept of abstraction. A function $\gamma: T \to T'$ is said to be an *abstraction* if and only if:

(*i*)   For any standard process $x = <e, p, e'>$ in T', there exists some structured task $U(e, e')$ in T such that $\gamma^{-1}[x] = U$.

(*ii*) For any auxiliary process y in T', $\gamma^{-1}[y] = \{y\}$.

A graphical illustration of an abstraction is shown in Figure 5.5.

Two important properties of abstractions are spelt out below. Theorem 5.3.1 shows that we can manipulate structured tasks using abstractions with the full confidence that structuredness will be preserved. Theorem 5.3.3 shows that the usual properties of continuous functions, such as those proposed in Fernandez (1975, 1976) and Genrich *et al.* (1980), apply also to abstractions. One important conclusion which we can draw directly, for instance, is that structured tasks together with abstraction functions form a category.

Theorem 5.3.1
An abstraction is a structured function.

Proof: Let γ be an abstraction. Consider an arbitrary structured task $V \subseteq T'$. It is the result of applying sequence, selection, iteration and parallel connection on elementary tasks $\{x_i\}$ in T, where each x_i is a standard process. For every x_i, $\gamma^{-1}[x_i]$ is a structured task in T. Thus $\gamma^{-1}[V]$ is the result of applying sequence, selection, iteration and parallel connection on structured tasks $\gamma^{-1}[x_i]$, and is therefore structured. ☐

Lemma 5.3.2
Any structured function is continuous.

Proof: Let $f: T \to T'$ be a structured function. We would like to prove that, for any open task $V \subseteq T'$, $f^{-1}[V] \subseteq T$ is open. By definition, V must of the form $\bigcup_i W_i$ where each W_i is a structured task. Hence $f^{-1}[V] = \bigcup_i f^{-1}[W_i]$. Since each $f^{-1}[W_i]$ is a structured task, $f^{-1}[V]$ is a union of structured tasks and is therefore open. ☐

Theorem 5.3.3
An abstraction is a continuous function.

Proof: The theorem follows directly from Theorem 5.3.1 and Lemma 5.3.2. ☐

Corollary 5.3.4
The set of processes together with abstraction morphisms form a category.

Proof: This follows directly from Theorem 5.3.3 and the result of Fernandez (1975). □

5.4 CATEGORY OF DeMARCO-LIKE TASKS

In structured methodologies, we are more interested in the refinement of structured tasks. This is formally defined through the category *Task*. As we have seen, tasks can be represented graphically using DeMarco-like data flow diagrams, and hence the name "DeMarco-like tasks".

(*a*) *Objects:* The objects of *Task* are structured tasks.

(*b*) *Morphisms:* We would like to define a refinement in *Task* as the inverse image $\gamma^{-1}[\_]$ of an abstraction in *Process*. Let 2^X denote the power set of any given set X. Given structured tasks T and T', a *refinement* in *Task* is a function $\lambda: 2^{T'} \rightarrow 2^T$ mapping tasks V (or subsets of T') to tasks U (or subsets of T) such that

$$U = \lambda(V) \text{ if and only if } U = \gamma^{-1}[V]. \; \dagger$$

In this case, U is also said to be a refinement of V. A graphical illustration of the refinement process is shown in Figure 5.6.

In this way, refinements help users to visualize the development of a systems specification. The sample specification in the last chapter, for instance, can be developed in terms of refinements. Thus, the process

$$x = \text{<<source customer, file customer-file>, process-sales, file invoice>}$$

can be refined to a task

$$V = \lambda(\{x\})$$
$$= \{ \text{<<source customer, file customer-file>, get-valid-order, valid-order>,}$$
$$\text{<valid-order, process-order, invoice-info>,}$$
$$\text{<invoice-info, put-invoice, file invoice>} \}$$

which can be further refined to another task

$$U = \lambda'(V)$$
$$= \{ \text{<<source customer, file customer-file>, get-order, order>,}$$
$$\text{<order, validate-order, valid-order>,}$$
$$\text{<valid-order, } \oplus, \text{ <bulk-order, regular-order>>,}$$
$$\text{<bulk-order, prepare-bulk, pre-bulk-info>,}$$
$$\text{<pre-bulk-info, calc-discount, bulk-info>,}$$

---

† The symbols γ and λ have been chosen for abstractions and refinements because of their graphical outlook. An abstraction γ is conceived as combining two streams (at the top) into one single stream (at the bottom). A refinement λ is conceived as separating a stream (at the top) into two (at the bottom).

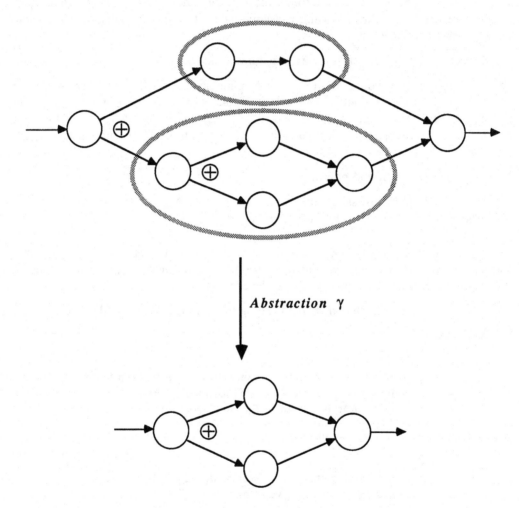

Abstraction γ

Figure 5.5 Graphical Illustration of Abstraction

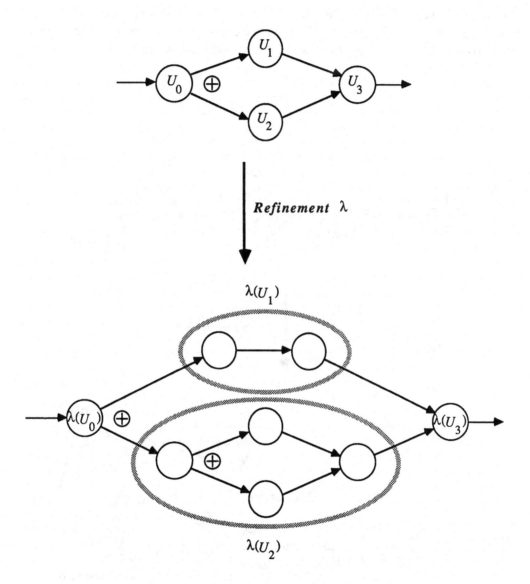

Figure 5.6 Graphical Illustration of Refinement

<regular-order, precess-regular, regular-info>,
<<bulk-info, regular-info>, O, invoice-info>,
<invoice-info, put-invoice, **file** invoice>}

and so on. Hence stepwise refinement can simply be conceived as a set-manipulation process, which can easily be aided by a computerized system. For the sake of user-friendliness, we can also represent the refinement steps diagrammatically, as shown in Figure 5.7.

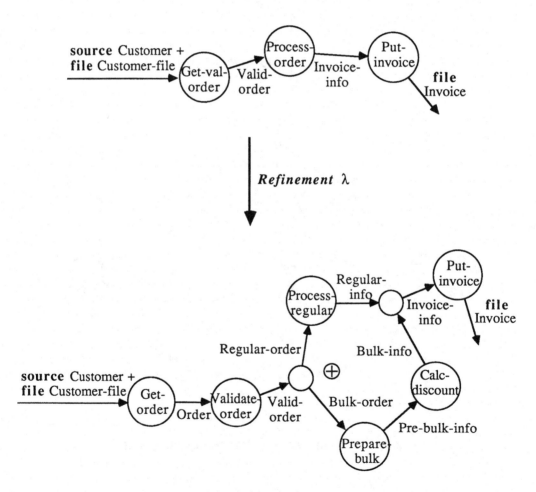

Figure 5.7 Example of Refinement in *Task*

5.5 OTHER CATEGORIES OF STRUCTURED MODELS

We define a category of terms, denoted by $\mathcal{T}\!erm$, as follows:

(a) *Objects:* We have defined in the last chapter an initial algebra which is made up of terms of various sorts. Not all the terms, however, are of equal importance to us. We are more interested in the terms related with the sort *task*, or in other words, terms which begin with the operation symbol **task**. We therefore define $|\mathcal{T}\!erm|$, the objects of $\mathcal{T}\!erm$, as terms in $(T_\Sigma)_{task}$.

(b) *Morphisms:* For any objects X and X' in $|\mathcal{T}\!erm|$, a refinement λ is a function mapping the set of all subterms in X to the set of subterms in X' and satisfying the following conditions:

   (i) Any elementary term $\mathbf{task}(p; e; e'; \mathbf{elem})$ is mapped either to itself or to some term of the form

$$\mathbf{task}(p; e; e'; \sigma(t_0; ...; t_n))$$

where σ is an operation symbol and $t_0, ..., t_n$ are further terms.

   (ii) Suppose the terms $u_0, ..., u_n$ are mapped to $v_0, ..., v_n$. Then a term of the form $\mathbf{task}(p; e; e'; \sigma(u_0; ...; u_n))$ is mapped to the term

$$\mathbf{task}(p; e; e'; \sigma(v_0; ...; v_n))$$

An example illustrating the objects and morphisms in the category $\mathcal{T}\!erm$ is shown in Figure 5.8.

If we modify our terms and refinements slightly, we can obtain other common structured models. For example, the category $\mathcal{T}\!erm$ can be modified to represent Yourdon structured charts by forgetting about sources and sinks, and equating parallel connections with sequences. It can also be modified to represent Jackson structure texts by forgetting about all input and output events, and again equating parallel connections with sequences. Abstractions can be defined in a similar fashion. Examples illustrating the categories $\mathcal{Y}ourdon$ and $\mathcal{J}ackson$ defined in this way are shown in Figures 5.9 and 5.10.

task (process-sales; **source** (customer) + **infile** (customer-file); **outfile** (invoice); **elem**)

Refinement λ

task (process-sales; **source** (customer) + **infile** (customer-file); **outfile** (invoice);
sequ (**task** (get-valid-order; **source** (customer) + **infile** (customer-file);
           outdata (valid-order); **elem**);
        task (**null**; **indata** (valid-order); **outfile** (invoice);
        sequ (**task** (process-order; **indata** (valid-order); **outdata** (invoice-info);
                  elem);
               task (put-invoice; **indata** (invoice-info); **outfile** (invoice); **elem**)))

Refinement λ'

task (process-sales; **source** (customer) + **infile** (customer-file); **outfile** (invoice);
sequ (**task** (get-valid-order; **source** (customer) + **infile** (customer-file);
           outdata (valid-order);
        sequ (**task** (get-order; **source** (customer) + **infile** (customer-file);
                  outdata (order); **elem**);
               task (validate-order; **indata** (order); **outdata** (valid-order); **elem**)));
        task (**null**; **indata** (valid-order); **outfile** (invoice);
        sequ (**task** (process-order; **indata** (valid-order); **outdata** (invoice-info);
                  seln (**task** (process-bulk; **indata** (bulk-order); **outdata** (bulk-info);
                        sequ (**task** (prepare-bulk; **indata** (bulk-order);
                                  outdata (pre-bulk-info); **elem**);
                               task (calc-discount; **indata** (pre-bulk-info);
                                  outdata (bulk-info); **elem**)));
                        task (process-regular; **indata** (regular-order);
                               outdata (regular-info); **elem**)));
               task (put-invoice; **indata** (invoice-info); **outfile** (invoice); **elem**)))))

Figure 5.8 Sample Morphisms in the Category *Term*

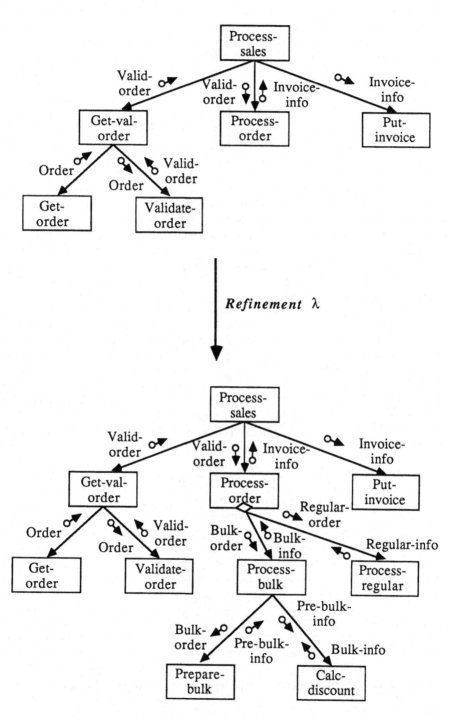

Figure 5.9 Sample Morphism in the Category *Yourdon*

process-sales

Refinement λ

process-sales **seq**
    get-valid-order;
    process-order;
    put-invoice
process-sales **end**

Refinement λ′

process-sales **seq**
    get-valid-order **seq**
        get-order;
        validate-order
    get-valid-order **end**;
    process-order **sel**
        process-bulk **seq**
            prepare-bulk;
            calc-discount
        process-bulk **end**;
    process-order **alt**
        process-regular
    process-order **end**;
    put-invoice
process-sales **end**

Figure 5.10 Sample Morphisms in the Category *Jackson*

5.6 FUNCTORS AND FREENESS

Since the structured models are slightly different ways of representing structured tasks, we would like to know whether there is any mapping which helps us to convert one representation to another. Functors, or functions which preserve the morphisms, can be defined between categories. A specification in the form of a term in the initial algebra, for example, can be mapped to a specification in the form of a DeMarco-like task diagram.

But the main difference between the initial algebraic and the functorial frameworks is not simply a matter of difference in mathematical notation. There are two fundamental differences. Firstly, as we have seen, the functorial framework allows us to perform stepwise refinements on incomplete specifications. When a specification is mapped from one form to another, the functors will preserve the refinement steps. Secondly, although the term algebra provides us with a model which has no junk and no confusion, users may not be happy to define their system in such a formal way. Users may prefer to specify a system in the form of a data flow diagram, convert it into initial algebra, and hence transform it further into other structured models. The reverse path is not catered for in the initial algebra framework defined in the last chapter. Using functors, however, terms can be freely generated from tasks in a data flow diagram.

For the purpose of illustration, we shall construct in this section a functor G which map the category *Term* to the category *Task*. We shall show that this functor has a left adjoint F. That is to say, there is free functor F mapping in the reverse direction such that, given an object Y in *Task*, there is a free object $F(Y)$ in *Term* such that for every λ, there is a unique λ' satisfying the commutative diagram shown in Figure 5.11.

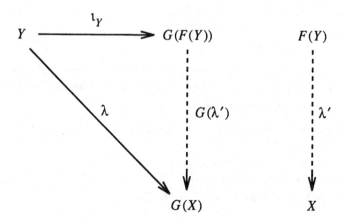

Figure 5.11 Functorial Relationship between *Task* and *Term*

To define a functor G: $\mathit{Term} \rightarrow \mathit{Task}$, let us first of all define $G(X)$ for any X in $|\mathit{Term}|$.

(a) Given any term $t = \mathbf{task}(p; e; e'; \mathbf{elem})$ in X, let $G(t) = \{<e, p, e'>\}$.

(b) Suppose $G(t_0)$ and $G(t_1)$ have been defined for t_0 and t_1 in X. Then

$$G(\mathbf{task}(p; e; e'; \mathbf{sequ}(t_0; t_1))) = (G(t_0) \bullet G(t_1))(e, e')$$
$$G(\mathbf{task}(p; e; e'; \mathbf{seln}(t_0; t_1))) = (G(t_0) \oplus G(t_1))(e, e')$$
$$G(\mathbf{task}(p; e; e'; \mathbf{para}(t_0; t_1))) = (G(t_0) \otimes G(t_1))(e, e')$$
$$G(\mathbf{task}(p; e; e'; \mathbf{iter}(t_0))) = *(G(t_0))(e, e')$$

In other words, the functor G helps us to forget about the intermediate processes involved in the terms. But the construction of a functor would not be complete until we have shown that it can preserve morphisms. For any refinement morphism λ' mapping a set of terms to another, we define $G(\lambda')$ as follows: †

(i) For any elementary task $U = \{<e_0, p, e_1>\}$ in $G(X)$, let

$$G\lambda'(U) = G(\lambda'(\mathbf{task}(p; e_0; e_1; \mathbf{elem})))$$

(ii) Suppose $G\lambda'(U)$ and $G\lambda'(V)$ have been defined for the structured tasks U and V in $G(X)$. Let

$$G\lambda'(U \bullet V) = G\lambda'(U) \bullet G\lambda'(V)$$
$$G\lambda'(U \oplus V) = G\lambda'(U) \oplus G\lambda'(V)$$
$$G\lambda'(U \otimes V) = G\lambda'(U) \otimes G\lambda'(V)$$
$$G\lambda'(*(U)) = *(G\lambda'(U))$$

The existence of a left adjoint for the functor G is given by the following theorem.

Theorem 5.6.1
There is a free functor F: $\mathit{Task} \rightarrow \mathit{Term}$.

Proof: We construct F as follows:

(a) For any structured task U, we define $F(U)$ to be the term freely generated from U by forgetting any of the intermediate processes in the refinement history. For instance, given the structured task

{<<**source** customer, **file** customer-file>, get-order, order>,
<order, validate-order, valid-order>,
<valid-order, ⊕, <bulk-order, regular-order>>,
<bulk-order, prepare-bulk, pre-bulk-info>,
<pre-bulk-info, calc-discount, bulk-info>,

---

† To avoid the excessive use of brackets, we shall denote $(G(\lambda'))(U)$ simply by $G\lambda'(U)$.

<regular-order, precess-regular, regular-info>,
<<bulk-info, regular-info>, O, invoice-info>,
<invoice-info, put-invoice, **file** invoice>}

the following term will be freely generated:

task(**null**; **source**(customer) + **infile**(customer-file); **outfile**(invoice);
sequ(**task**(**null**; **source**(customer) + **infile**(customer-file);
    outdata(valid-order);
    sequ(**task**(get-order; **source**(customer) + **infile**(customer-file);
        outdata(order); **elem**);
        task(validate-order; **indata**(order); **outdata**(valid-order);
        elem)));
task(**null**; **indata**(valid-order); **outfile**(invoice);
sequ(**task**(**null**; **indata**(valid-order); **outdata**(invoice-info);
    seln(**task**(**null**; **indata**(bulk-order); **outdata**(bulk-info);
        sequ(**task**(prepare-bulk; **indata**(bulk-order);
            outdata(pre-bulk-info); **elem**);
            task(calc-discount; **indata**(pre-bulk-info);
            outdata(bulk-info); **elem**)));
        task(process-regular; **indata**(regular-order);
            outdata(regular-info); **elem**)));
    task(put-invoice; **indata**(invoice-info); **outfile**(invoice);
    elem)))))

(b) We define $\iota_Y: Y \to G(F(Y))$ such that $\iota_Y(U) = U$ for any U in Y.

To prove F is free functor, we need only show that, given an arbitrary set of terms X and any morphism $\lambda: Y \to G(X)$, we can construct a unique morphism $\lambda': F(Y) \to X$ which makes Figure 5.11 commute. Indeed, given any λ, we can define λ' recursively thus:

(i) For any elementary term $t = $ **task**$(p; e; e';$ **elem**$)$ in $F(Y)$, let

$$\lambda'(t) = F(\lambda(\{<e, p, e'>\})).$$

(ii) Suppose $t'_0 = \lambda'(t_0), ..., t'_n = \lambda'(t_n)$ for $t_0, ..., t_n$ in $F(Y)$. Let

$$\lambda'(\textbf{task}(p; e; e'; \sigma(t_0; ...; t_n))) = \textbf{task}(p; e; e'; \sigma(t'_0; ...; t'_n))$$

Then:

(a) For any elementary task U in Y,

$$G\lambda'(\iota_Y(U)) = G\lambda'(U) = G(\lambda'(t)) = G(F(\lambda(U))) = \lambda(U)$$

(b) For any tasks U and V in Y such that $G\lambda'(\iota_Y(U)) = \lambda(U)$ and $G\lambda'(\iota_Y(V)) = \lambda(V)$,

$$G\lambda'(\iota_Y(U \bullet V)) = G\lambda'(U \bullet V) = G\lambda'(U) \bullet G\lambda'(V) = \lambda(U) \bullet \lambda(V)$$
$$= \lambda(U \bullet V)$$
$$G\lambda'(\iota_Y(U \oplus V)) = G\lambda'(U \oplus V) = G\lambda'(U) \oplus G\lambda'(V) = \lambda(U) \oplus \lambda(V)$$
$$= \lambda(U \oplus V)$$
$$G\lambda'(\iota_Y(U \otimes V)) = G\lambda'(U \otimes V) = G\lambda'(U) \otimes G\lambda'(V) = \lambda(U) \otimes \lambda(V)$$
$$= \lambda(U \otimes V)$$
$$G\lambda'(\iota_Y(*V)) = G\lambda'(*V) = *(G\lambda'(V)) = *(\lambda(V)) = \lambda(*(V))$$

Hence Figure 5.11 is commutative.

Assume that there exists another morphism λ'' ($\neq \lambda'$) satisfying Figure 5.11. In this case, one of (*i*) or (*ii*) above is not satisfied. If (*i*) is false, then there exists some elementary term $t = \mathbf{task}(p; e; e'; \mathbf{elem})$ in $F(Y)$ such that

$$\lambda'(t) \neq F(\lambda(\{<e, p, e'>\}))$$

Let $U = \{<e, p, e'>\}$. Then

$$G\lambda'(\iota_Y(U)) = G\lambda'(U) \neq G(F(\lambda(U))) = \lambda(U)$$

which contradicts Figure 5.11. If (*ii*) is false, it contradicts our definition of morphisms in *Term*. Hence λ' must be unique. □

We can also define a forgetful functor from *Term* to *Yourdon*, by mapping parallel connections into sequences and ignoring sources and sinks in terms. We can define left inverse functors in the opposite direction, but they are not unique. In other words, the forgetful functor from *Term* to *Yourdon* does not have a left adjoint. Similarly, we can define a forgetful functor from *Term* to *Jackson* and left inverse functors in the reversed direction. The overall picture is given in Figure 5.1.

In this way, we can integrate the models by providing functorial bridges from one type of specification to another. We see that the initial algebra as proposed in the last chapter is only part of a more general framework for linking up the structured analysis and design models. Terms in the initial algebra, for example, can be mapped to DeMarco-like task diagrams or Yourdon structure charts. Conversely, terms in the initial algebra can be generated freely from DeMarco-like task diagrams.

5.7 CONCLUSION

A functorial framework is proposed in this chapter to link up the structured analysis and design models. The concepts of structured tasks and refinements are defined. They help a systems developer to visualize the internal structure of a system, assemble or refine subsystems, and verify the consistency and completeness of a design. These can be done through simple set-manipulations with DeMarco-like task diagrams as a visual aid.

The structured tasks together with refinements form a category. Similar categories can be defined over other structured models such as Yourdon structure charts and Jackson structure texts. Even the term algebra which we proposed in the last chapter can be regarded as a category. We can integrate the models by providing functorial bridges from one type of specification to another. Terms in the initial algebra can be generated freely from DeMarco-like task diagrams. The terms can be further mapped to Yourdon structure charts or Jackson structure texts.

6 The Identification of Unstructuredness

6.1 INTRODUCTION

In this chapter, we shall give a further illustration of the theoretical usefulness of our framework by applying it in the identification of unstructuredness. Since DeMarco data flow diagrams are mainly used as communication tools with users during the analysis stage of systems development, they are problem-oriented and probably unstructured. Some mechanism must be available enabling us to detect the unstructured elements so that we can construct structured tasks and define refinement morphisms accordingly. We shall extend our concepts in tasks and show that only one single criterion is necessary and sufficient for identifying unstructuredness. Looking at it in another way, a single criterion is necessary and sufficient for proving a task to be structured.

Quite a number of papers have already addressed a similar problem of detecting unstructuredness in program schemes and transforming the schemes into structured equivalents. These papers can roughly be classified as follows:

(a) Most of the papers are based on heuristic arguments (Colter 1985, McCabe 1976, Mills 1972, Oulsman 1982, Williams 1977, Williams and Ossher 1978, Williams and Chen 1985). Each paper gives a new proposal supposedly better than earlier ones (Prather and Giulieri 1981). According to the arguments in McCabe (1976), Oulsman (1982), Williams (1977) and Williams and Ossher (1978), unstructuredness may be due to any of four elements — branching out of a loop, branching into a loop, branching out of a selection and branching into a selection. The identification of these elements, however, has remained a difficult task. Since unstructured elements cannot exist in isolation, the authors recommend that we should identify unstructured compounds, or combinations of unstructured elements. Unfortunately, the number of combinations is endless, so that we can never exhaust all the possible cases (Williams 1983).

(b) The second approach uses the concept of reducibility of program schemes (Cowell et al. 1980, Greibach 1975, Kosaraju 1974, Prather and Giulieri 1981, Williams 1982). In essence, a program scheme U_0 is reducible to another scheme U_1 if and only if U_0 can be transformed to U_1 according to some defined rules. A program scheme will be structured if it can be reduced to a structured scheme, which consists only of sequences, selections and while-loops. It will not be structured if irreducible forms are encountered. In practice, however, the number of irreducible forms increases exponentially with the number of decision nodes in a scheme

(Cowell *et al.* 1980). As a result, it will be quite difficult to decide on the reducibility of large program schemes.

(*c*) A third approach makes use of the concept of succession paths in flowgraphs to define the module related to a given node. This is more promising because it produces simple but working algorithms. For example, an efficient algorithm is proposed in Urschler (1975) to restructure programs automatically. However, since no attempt has been made to identify unstructuredness, one may spend a lot of time restructuring programs which are already structured. The approach is re-examined in Becerril *et al.* (1980) in the context of formal language theory. Unfortunately, no less than nine non-trivial errors are found in the paper, so that the proposed theorems are unreliable.

Because of the problems of the first two approaches and the promise of the third, we shall study the conditions for structuredness of tasks in terms of succession paths. We shall show that only one single criterion is necessary and sufficient for the identification of unstructuredness. In Sections 6.2 and 6.3, the concepts of elementary succession paths, least common successors, skeletons and minimal subtasks will be introduced. Then unstructuredness will be formally defined in Section 6.4. In particular, multiple exits in iterations will be studied in more detail in Section 6.5. Finally, the concepts of fully embedded skeletons and partially overlapping skeletons will be introduced in Section 6.6, so that a necessary and sufficient condition for unstructuredness can be proved. Only a knowledge of elementary set theory will be assumed. Theorems in graph theory or partially ordered sets will not be used in the proofs.

We shall illustrate our theorems through a common example, as shown in Figure 6.1. The example has been chosen to show all the features of unstructuredness. In a task diagram such as this, readers may easily be confused because of the over-abundance of process names p_i and input/output events e_j. To improve the situation, we have redrawn the task diagram and put labels only on the processes. The simplified task diagram is shown in Figure 6.2. This figure will be quoted throughout the chapter for illustration.

6.2 CONNECTED TASKS AND SKELETONS

A task U is said to have *a single entry and a single exit* if and only if it satisfies the following conditions:

(*a*) U is a finite set of standard or auxiliary processes.

(*b*) There exists one and only one process with one and only one input event e_{begin} such that no process in U has e_{begin} as its output. Furthermore, given any other event e, we can find one and only one process in U having e as its output.

(*c*) There exists one and only one process with one and only one output event e_{end} such that no process in U has e_{end} as its input. Furthermore, given any other

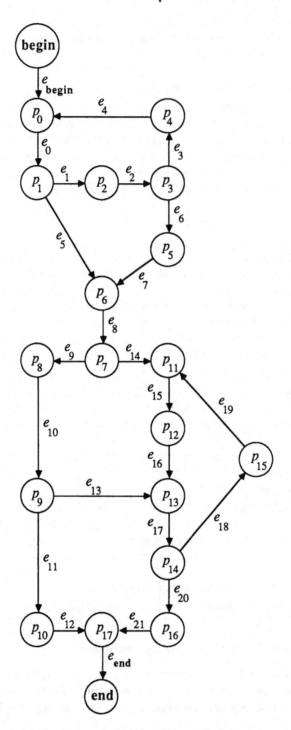

Figure 6.1 Example of an Unstructured Task

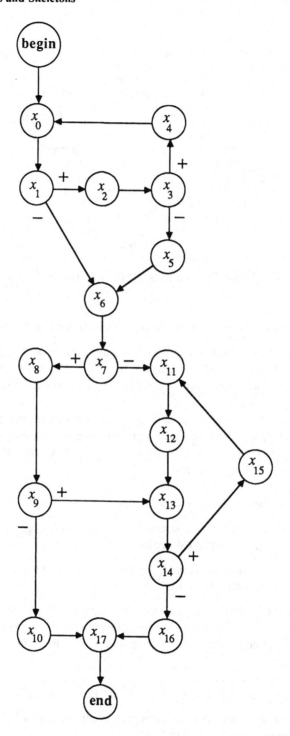

Figure 6.2 Example of an Unstructured Task using Simplified Notation

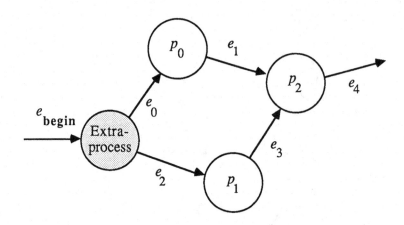

Figure 6.3 Adding Extra Process to form Single Entry in Task

event e, we can find one and only one process in U having e as its input.

For example, the task in Figure 6.1 has only a single entry and a single exit. If we encounter a task with more than one entry or exit, we can easily link them together through extra forks or joins. A simple example is shown in Figure 6.3.

Given a task with a single entry and a single exit, we can divide the processes into two classes: *simplexes*, which have one output event each, and *duplexes*, which have two output events each. For example, standard processes and joins are simplexes, whereas decisions and forks are duplexes.

Furthermore, let us construct two more processes:

(a) A process with no input event and only one output event e_{begin}. It is denoted by $<\Lambda, \textbf{begin}, e_{begin}>$, or simply by **begin**.

(b) A process with one input event e_{end} but no output event. It is denoted by $<e_{end}, \textbf{end}, \Lambda>$, or simply by **end**.

We shall extend the task with a single entry and a single exit to include the **begin** and **end** processes. The task in Figure 6.2, for instance, has been extended in this way. For simplicity, the extended task $U \cup \{\textbf{begin}, \textbf{end}\}$ will simply be written as U throughout this chapter.

Successor functions $s_+ : U \to U$ and $s_- : U \to U$ are defined on a task U as follows:

(a) If x is a simplex in U and if e is its output event, then e will be the input event for a unique process y in U. We define

$$s_+(x) = s_-(x) = y$$

(b) If x is a duplex in U and if e and e' are its output events, then e and e' will be the input event for unique processes y and w in U. We define

$$s_+(x) = y$$
$$s_-(x) = w$$

(c) If x is a join, then the inverse image $s_+^{-1}[x]$ consists of two processes. If x is some other process, then $s_+^{-1}[x]$ consists of only one process. The inverse image for $s_-^{-1}[x]$ is similar.

The processes $s_+(x)$ and $s_-(x)$ are known in general as the *immediate successors* of the process x. The subscripts "+" and "−" are known as the *directions* of the immediate successors. We shall use Greek letters α, β and so on to denote directions, and use $-\alpha$, $-\beta$ and so forth to denote the respective opposite directions. We shall regard **end** as a simplex and **begin** as a duplex by defining

$$s_+(\textbf{end}) = \textbf{end}$$
$$s_-(\textbf{end}) = \textbf{end}$$
$$s_+(\textbf{begin}) = v$$
$$s_-(\textbf{begin}) = \textbf{end}$$

where v is the process having $e_{\textbf{begin}}$ as its input event.

Our concept of succession is equivalent to the concepts of dominance in Prather and Giulieri (1981), postdominance in Becerril *et al.* (1980) and Urschler (1975), back dominance in Greibach (1975), reverse dominance in Williams (1982) and descendants in Tarjan (1972). The term "succession" has been deliberately chosen in order to avoid the controversy (Williams 1982) towards the possible meanings of the term "dominance".

Given a task with one entry and one exit, we cannot guarantee that there is indeed a path leading from $e_{\textbf{begin}}$ to $e_{\textbf{end}}$. A simple illustration is shown in Figure 6.4. We need the concept of a *connected task*, which is defined as a task with a single entry and a single exit satisfying the following condition:

> For any process x other than **end**, there exist a finite sequence of processes $<y_0, \ldots, y_n, \textbf{end}>$ and a finite sequence of directions $<\beta_0, \ldots, \beta_n>$ such that
>
> $$y_0 = x$$
> $$y_i = s_{\beta_{i-1}}(y_{i-1}) \text{ for } i = 1, \ldots, n$$
> $$\textbf{end} = y_n$$

The above sequence of processes is known as a *succession path*. It is called an *elementary succession path* if and only if it does not contain more than one occurrence of the same process. A process y is known as a *common successor* of another process x if and only if all the elementary succession paths $<s_+(x), \ldots, \textbf{end}>$ and $<s_-(x), \ldots,$

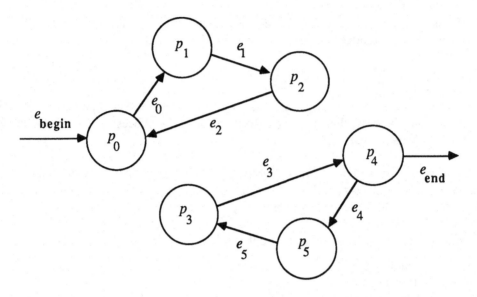

Figure 6.4 Example of an Unconnected Task

end> contain y. In this case we write $x < y$. Furthermore, we shall borrow the standard mathematical shorthand "$\leq$" to denote "$<$ or $=$". Thus $x \leq y$ means, effectively, that (a) all elementary succession paths from x lead us to y, or (b) we are already there. In Figure 6.2, for instance, we have

$$\textbf{begin} \leq x_0 \leq x_6 \leq x_7 \leq x_{17} \leq \textbf{end}$$
$$x_{15} \leq x_{11} \leq x_{12} \leq x_{13} \leq x_{14} \leq x_{16} \leq x_{17} \leq \textbf{end}$$

The *least common successor* of x, denoted by $s_\perp(x)$, is a process such that

(a) $x < s_\perp(x)$

(b) For any process y, $x < y$ implies $s_\perp(x) \leq y$.

The least common successor of a simplex is its immediate successor and the least common successor of **begin** is **end**. The least common successor of any process in general can be found using depth first search (Aho *et al.* 1983, Tarjan 1972). In our example,

$$s_\perp(x_0) = x_1$$
$$s_\perp(x_3) = x_6$$
$$s_\perp(x_7) = x_{17}$$
$$s_\perp(x_{14}) = x_{16}$$

Given a process x and a direction α, if $s_\alpha(x) = s_\perp(x)$, we define the *skeleton* $q_\alpha(x)$ as the empty sequence Λ. Otherwise we define $q_\alpha(x)$ as the sequence of processes $\langle y_0, ..., y_n \rangle$ such that

$$y_0 = s_\alpha(x)$$
$$y_i = s_\perp(y_{i-1}) \text{ for } i = 1, ..., n \text{ (if } s_\perp(x) \neq s_\perp(y_0))$$
$$s_\perp(x) = s_\perp(y_n)$$

The skeletons for some of the processes in Figure 6.2 are as follows:

$$q_+(x_0) = q_-(x_0) = \Lambda$$
$$q_+(x_7) = <x_8, x_9>$$
$$q_-(x_7) = <x_{11}, x_{12}, x_{13}, x_{14}, x_{16}>$$
$$q_+(x_{14}) = <x_{15}, x_{11}, x_{12}, x_{13}, x_{14}>$$
$$q_-(x_{14}) = \Lambda$$

In general, the skeletons of simplexes are empty, and the properties of the skeletons of duplexes will be spelt out in the following lemmas and proposition.

Lemma 6.2.1
Given a process x, if one of its skeletons $q_\alpha(x)$ is non-empty, there exists an elementary succession path $<x, s_{-\alpha}(x), ..., \textbf{end}>$.

Proof: The lemma is trivial if x is a simplex. Suppose x is a duplex. Assume that no elementary succession path from x passes through $s_{-\alpha}(x)$. Then all elementary succession paths from x pass through $s_\alpha(x)$, and hence $x < s_\alpha(x)$. Therefore, by definition of least common successor, $s_\perp(x) \leq s_\alpha(x)$. But since $s_\alpha(x)$ immediately follows x, we must have $s_\perp(x) = s_\alpha(x)$. In other words, $q_\alpha(x)$ would be empty. $\square$

Lemma 6.2.2
Given a process x, any elementary succession path $<s_\alpha(x), ..., \textbf{end}>$ contains all the elements of the corresponding skeleton $q_\alpha(x)$.

Proof: The lemma is trivial if $q_\alpha(x)$ is empty. Suppose it is non-empty. Let $q_\alpha(x) = <y_0, ..., y_n>$. Then

$$y_0 = s_\alpha(x)$$
$$y_i = s_\perp(y_{i-1}) \text{ for } i = 1, ..., n \text{ (if } q_\perp(x) \neq q_\perp(y_0))$$

Hence $y_0 \leq ... \leq y_n \leq s_\perp(x) \leq \textbf{end}$ $\square$

Based on these two lemmas, we can derive the next proposition.

Proposition 6.2.3
Given any process x, if one of its skeletons $q_\alpha(x)$ contains x, then the opposite skeleton $q_{-\alpha}(x)$ must be empty.

Proof: Assume the contrary. By Lemma 6.2.1, there exists an elementary succession path $<x, s_\alpha(x), ..., \textbf{end}>$. But by Lemma 6.2.2, x is in $<s_\alpha(x), ..., \textbf{end}>$. This contradicts the definition of elementary succession paths. $\square$

For instance, since the skeleton $q_+(x_{14})$ in Figure 6.2 contains x_{14}, the opposite skeleton $q_-(x_{14})$ must be empty.

6.3 MINIMAL SUBTASKS

For any process x in a task, we define the *minimal subtask containing* x (or simply the *subtask* $U(x)$) as a subset of the task which satisfy the following conditions:

(a) x is in $U(x)$

(b) Given any process y in $U(x)$, all the processes in both the skeletons $q_+(y)$ and $q_-(y)$ are in $U(x)$

(c) No other process is in $U(x)$.

The subtask $U(\textbf{begin})$ consists of the entire task minus the **end** process. Further examples can be found in Figure 6.2, thus:

$$U(x_0) = \{x_0\}$$
$$U(x_7) = \{x_7, x_8, x_9, x_{10}, x_{11}, x_{12}, x_{13}, x_{14}, x_{15}, x_{16}\}$$
$$U(x_{14}) = \{x_{11}, x_{12}, x_{13}, x_{14}, x_{15}\}$$

This simple definition of subtasks avoids the lengthly treatment of "modules" in Becerril *et al.* (1980).

In general, we can decide whether any process is inside a given subtask using the following proposition.

Proposition 6.3.1

Given a process x, another process y ($\neq x$) is in the subtask $U(x)$ if and only if there exists a finite sequence of skeletons $<q_{\delta_0}(w_0), ..., q_{\delta_n}(w_n)>$ such that

$$y \in q_{\delta_0}(w_0)$$
$$w_{i-1} \in q_{\delta_i}(w_i) \text{ for } i = 1, ..., n \text{ (if } y \notin q_+(x) \text{ and } q_-(x))$$
$$w_n = x$$

Proof: Suppose y ($\neq x$) is a process in $U(x)$. Then $y \neq s_\perp(x)$. By definition, there exists a process w_0 in $U(x)$ such that one of its skeletons $q_{\delta_0}(w_0)$ contains y. If $w_0 \neq x$, there exists a process w_1 in $U(x)$ such that one of its skeletons $q_{\delta_1}(w_1)$ contains w_0. Since $U(x)$ is a subset of the task, it contains only a finite number of processes. We can therefore reach x by applying the above procedure a finite number of times. Hence there exists a finite sequence of skeletons $<q_{\delta_0}(w_0), ..., q_{\delta_n}(w_n)>$ such that

$$y \in q_{\delta_0}(w_0)$$
$$w_{i-1} \in q_{\delta_i}(w_i) \text{ for } i = 1, \ldots, n \text{ (if } y \notin q_+(x) \text{ and } q_-(x))$$
$$w_n = x$$

Let us prove the converse. Suppose there is a finite sequence of skeletons $<q_{\delta_0}(w_0)$, $\ldots, q_{\delta_n}(w_n)>$ satisfying the above conditions. Since $U(x)$ contains w_n and $q_{\delta_n}(w_n)$ contains w_{n-1}, $U(x)$ must contain w_{n-1}. Proceeding in this way for a finite number of steps, we can conclude that $U(x)$ contains y. $\square$

Given a process x in a task and given a direction α, we define a *branch* $B_\alpha(x)$ as a subset of the task which satisfies the following conditions:

(a) All the processes in the skeleton $q_\alpha(x)$ are in $B_\alpha(x)$

(b) Given a process y in $B_\alpha(x)$, all the processes in $U(y)$ are in $B_\alpha(x)$

(c) No other process is in $B_\alpha(x)$

For example, in Figure 6.2,

$$B_+(x_0) = B_-(x_0) = \varnothing$$
$$B_+(x_7) = \{x_8, x_9, x_{10}, x_{13}, x_{14}, x_{16}\}$$
$$B_-(x_7) = \{x_{11}, x_{12}, x_{13}, x_{14}, x_{15}, x_{16}\}$$
$$B_+(x_{14}) = \{x_{11}, x_{12}, x_{13}, x_{14}, x_{15}\}$$
$$B_-(x_{14}) = \varnothing$$

This simple definition of branches avoids the erroneous concept of "heads" in Becerril *et al.* (1980).

Similar to Proposition 6.3.1, the following is useful in deciding whether or not a process appears in a given branch.

Proposition 6.3.2
Given a process x, a process y is in the branch $B_\alpha(x)$ if and only if there exists a finite sequence of skeletons $<q_{\delta_0}(w_0), \ldots, q_{\delta_n}(w_n)>$ such that

$$y \in q_{\delta_0}(w_0)$$
$$w_{i-1} \in q_{\delta_i}(w_i) \text{ for } i = 1, \ldots, n \text{ (if } y \notin q_\alpha(x))$$
$$w_n = x$$
$$\delta_n = \alpha$$

Proof: The proof follows immediately from Proposition 6.3.1. $\square$

Given a process y inside a subtask $U(x)$, the minimal subtask $U(y)$ which contains y is of course a subset of $U(x)$. But we are also interested in finding out the condition for which the subtask $U(x)$ coincides with the minimal subtask $U(y)$. This is given by Corollary 6.3.5 of Proposition 6.3.4 below.

Lemma 6.3.3
If a process y is in the branch $B_\alpha(x)$, then the subtask $U(y)$ is a subset of $B_\alpha(x)$.

Proposition 6.3.4
Given a process y in a subtask $U(x)$, if a branch $B_\beta(y)$ of y contains x, then $U(y) = U(x)$.

Corollary 6.3.5
Given a process y in a subtask $U(x)$, if a skeleton $q_\beta(y)$ of y contains x, then $U(y) = U(x)$.

Proofs: The proofs of the above are obvious. ☐

6.4 DEFINING UNSTRUCTUREDNESS
As pointed out in Kosaraju (1974) and Williams (1983), there are several ways of defining structuredness. Hence the concept of unstructuredness also varies. In particular, it depends on whether do-until loops and n+half loops (Knuth 1974) are regarded as structured elements. We shall regard sequences, selections, parallel connections and do-while loops as structured, but consider other types of loops as unstructured. A connected task is defined as *unstructured* if and only if it contains at least one of the following:

(*a*) an entry in the middle of an iteration, selection or parallel connection
(*b*) an exit in the middle of a selection or parallel connection
(*c*) non-unique exit in an iteration.

Before we formally define unstructuredness in the following sections, we must define the concepts of entries, iteration, selection and parallel connection. Let x be a duplex. The subtask $U(x)$ is said to be an *iterative subtask* if and only if one of the branches $B_\alpha(x)$ contains x. Otherwise it is said to be a *non-iterative subtask*. A process y in the subtask $U(x)$ is said to be an *entry* of $U(x)$ if and only if y is not a join and there exist a process w outside $U(x)$ and a sequence of joins $<t_0, ..., t_n>$ in $U(x)$ such that

$$t_0 = s_\delta(w)$$
$$t_i = s_\perp(t_{i-1}) \text{ for } i = 1, ..., n \text{ (if } y \neq s_\perp(t_0))$$
$$y = s_\perp(t_n)$$

As we shall see later on in this chapter, joins only play an auxiliary role not just in the definition of entries but also in the study of unstructuredness in general. In order to distinguish between joins and other processes, we shall, for the sake of convenience, call the latter *non-trivial processes*.

The following property of entries will be useful for our main theorems in Section 6.6.

Proposition 6.4.1
If y is an entry of $U(x)$, there exists a process w outside $U(x)$ such that y is in $q_\delta(w)$.

Proof: Suppose y is an entry of $U(x)$. Then there exist a process w_0 outside $U(x)$ and a sequence of joins $<t_0, ..., t_n>$ in $U(x)$ such that

$$t_0 = s_{\delta_0}(w_0)$$
$$t_i = s_\perp(t_{i-1}) \text{ for } i = 1, ..., n \text{ (if } y \neq s_\perp(t_0))$$
$$y = s_\perp(t_n)$$

If w_0 is a duplex, then $q_{\delta_0}(w_0)$ contains y. If, on the other hand, w_0 is a simplex, then $t_0 = s_\perp(w_0)$, and there exists a process w_1 outside $U(x)$ such that one of its skeletons $q_{\delta_1}(w_1)$ contains w_0. If $s_\perp(y) \leq s_\perp(w_1)$, then $q_{\delta_1}(w_1)$ contains y. Otherwise $t_0 = s_\perp(w_1)$, and there exists another process w_2 outside $U(x)$ such that one of its skeletons $q_{\delta_2}(w_2)$ contains w_1. Proceeding in this way, since a task is finite, we can arrive at some process w_m outside $U(x)$ such that one of its skeletons $q_{\delta_s}(w_m)$ contains y. $\square$

6.4.1 An Entry in the Middle of a Selection or Parallel Connection
A process y is said to be an *entry in the middle of a selection or parallel connection* if and only if $y \neq x$ but is an entry of the non-iterative subtask $U(x)$. The process x_{14} in Figure 6.2 is one example.

6.4.2 An Exit in the Middle of a Selection or Parallel Connection
Intuitively, exits in the middle of selections or parallel connections may consist of the cases shown in Figure 6.5. On closer examination, however, we notice that case (c) turns the "non-iterative" subtask into an iterative subtask with multiple exits, and that case (b) is, in fact, topologically equivalent to (a). We shall therefore define exits in the middle of selections or parallel connections in terms of (a) only. A non-iterative subtask $U(x)$ is said to have an *exit in the middle* if and only if its branches $B_\alpha(x)$ and $B_{-\alpha}(x)$ have at least one non-trivial process in common. $U(x_7)$ of Figure 6.2 is an example of such a subtask.

6.4.3 An Entry in the Middle of an Iteration
Let y be a normal entry to an iterative subtask $U(x)$. Then y must either be x (in the case of do-while) or a non-trivial successor of x (in the case of repeat-until). An entry in any other form, or the existence of more than one entry, will imply that there is an

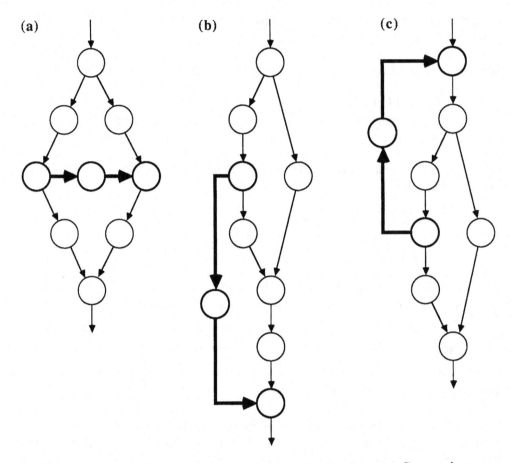

Figure 6.5 An Exit in the Middle of a Selection or Parallel Connection

entry in the middle of an iteration. More formally, an entry y is a *normal entry* if and only if $y = x$ or there exists a sequence of joins $<t_0, ..., t_n>$ such that

$$t_0 = s_+(x) \text{ or } s_-(x)$$
$$t_i = s_\perp(t_{i-1}) \text{ for } i = 1, ..., n \text{ (if } y \neq s_\perp(t_0))$$
$$y = s_\perp(t_n)$$

An entry y is said to be an *entry in the middle of an iteration* if and only if:

(a) y is not a normal entry, or
(b) there exists some other normal entry $\neq y$.

The process x_{12} in Figure 6.2, for instance, is not a normal entry but an entry in the middle of an iteration.

6.4.4 Non-Unique Exit in an Iteration

A process x is defined as an *exit of an iterative subtask* $U(y)$ if and only if:

(a) $U(x) = U(y)$

(b) x is in one of its own branches $B_\alpha(x)$ but not in the opposite branch $B_{-\alpha}(x)$.

An iterative subtask is said to have *multiple exits* if and only if it has more than one exit. For example, there are two exits x_1 and x_3 in the subtask $U(x_3)$ in Figure 6.2. On the other hand, an iterative subtask is said to have *no exit* if and only if its sole exit is a fork. The criterion for identifying multiple exits will be studied in the next section. The criterion for no exit will be a straightforward corollary.

6.5 IDENTIFICATION OF MULTIPLE ITERATION EXITS

In this section, we shall derive a sufficient and necessary condition for the identification of multiple iteration exits.

> **Lemma 6.5.1**
>
> If a process x is in one of its own branches $B_\alpha(x)$ and if an elementary succession path $<x, s_\alpha(x), ..., \textbf{end}>$ exists, then there is another process y in $B_\alpha(x)$ such that y is an iteration exit of the subtask $U(x)$.

Proof: By Proposition 6.3.2, since x is in $B_\alpha(x)$, there exists a finite sequence of skeletons $<q_{\beta_0}(y_0), ..., q_{\beta_n}(y_n)>$ such that

$$x \in q_{\beta_0}(y_0)$$
$$y_{i-1} \in q_{\beta_i}(y_i) \text{ for } i = 1, ..., n \text{ (if } x \notin q_\alpha(x))$$
$$y_n = x$$
$$\beta_n = \alpha$$

Obviously, the elementary succession path $<x, s_\alpha(x), ..., \textbf{end}>$ contains y_n but not y_0. In general, from Lemma 6.2.2, if the path contains $s_{\beta_i}(y_i)$, it will also contain y_{i-1}. Hence there exists some process y_j such that the path contains y_j but not the corresponding $s_{\beta_j}(y_j)$. For convenience, we shall denote this y_j by y and denote the corresponding β_j by β. Clearly $y \neq x$.

By Proposition 6.3.1, $U(y) = U(x)$. By Proposition 6.3.2, $B_\beta(y)$ contains y. We need only prove that $B_{-\beta}(y)$ does not contain y. Assume the contrary. By Lemma 6.3.3, $B_{-\beta}(y)$ also contains x. By Proposition 6.3.2, there exists a sequence of skeletons $<q_{\delta_0}(w_0), ..., q_{\delta_s}(w_m)>$ such that

$$x \in q_{\delta_0}(w_0)$$
$$w_{k-1} \in q_{\delta_k}(w_k) \text{ for } k = 1, ..., s \text{ (if } x \notin q_{-\beta}(y))$$
$$w_m = y$$

$$\delta_s = -\beta$$

Let w denote w_{m-1} if $s > 1$ and let it denote x otherwise. By Lemma 6.2.2, since w is in $q_{-\beta}(y)$, it lies on the elementary succession path $<x, s_\alpha(x), ..., \mathbf{end}>$. If $w = w_{m-1}$, this contradicts our earlier construction that $s_\beta(y)$ is not in the path. If $w = x$, it contradicts the definition of elementary succession paths. $\square$

Lemma 6.5.2

If a process x is in one of its own branches $B_\alpha(x)$ and if an elementary succession path $<x, s_\alpha(x), ..., \mathbf{end}>$ exists, then the subtask $U(x)$ contains multiple iteration exits.

Proof: By Lemma 6.5.1, there exists an iteration exit y ($\neq x$) in $B_\alpha(x)$. If $B_{-\alpha}(x)$ is empty, then x is a second exit. Suppose $B_{-\alpha}(x)$ is not empty. By Lemma 6.2.1, there exists an elementary path $<x, s_{-\alpha}(x), ..., \mathbf{end}>$. By Lemma 6.5.1, therefore, there exists an iteration exit w in $B_{-\alpha}(x)$. Assume that $U(x)$ contains only one exit. Then $y = w$, through which all the elementary succession paths will pass. Hence $s_\perp(x) \leq y \neq s_\perp(y) \leq s_\perp(x)$, which is a contradiction. $\square$

The next proposition therefore follows:

Proposition 6.5.3

If a process x is the only iteration exit of the subtask $U(x)$, then one of its skeletons $q_\alpha(x)$ must be empty.

Proof: By definition, x is in one of the branches $B_\alpha(x)$ but not in the opposite branch $B_{-\alpha}(x)$. Hence $q_\alpha(x)$ cannot be empty. Assume that $q_{-\alpha}(x)$ is also non-empty. By Lemma 6.2.1, there exists an elementary succession path $<x, s_\alpha(x), ..., \mathbf{end}>$. By Lemma 6.5.2, therefore, we have at least two iteration exits. $\square$

For example, since x_{14} of Figure 6.2 is the only iteration exit of the subtask $U(x_{14})$, we have $q_-(x_{14}) = \emptyset$. The reverse may not be true. The skeleton $q_-(x_1)$ is also empty but the subtask $U(x_1)$ has more than one exit.

We want to derive a necessary and sufficient condition for the presence of a unique iteration exit in a subtask. Let us first of all derive the following theorem:

Theorem 6.5.4

If a process x is the only iteration exit in the subtask $U(x)$, then one of its skeletons $q_\alpha(x)$ must contain x.

Proof: By Proposition 6.5.3, one of the branches $B_\alpha(x)$ contains x but the opposite branch $B_{-\alpha}(x)$ is empty. By the definition of branches, there exists a process y in $B_\alpha(x)$ such that a skeleton $q_\beta(y)$ of y contains x. Assume that $y \neq x$. By Corollary

6.3.5, $U(y) = U(x)$. Since x is the only iteration exit, y must be in both $B_\beta(y)$ and $B_{-\beta}(y)$.

By Lemma 6.2.1, since $B_\beta(y)$ is not empty, there exists an elementary succession path from y through $s_{-\beta}(y)$. By Lemma 6.5.1, there exists an iteration exit w in $B_{-\beta}(y)$. Since x is the only iteration exit, we must have $w = x$. Hence all elementary succession paths $<y, s_{-\beta}(y), ..., \mathbf{end}>$ pass through x. By a similar argument, all elementary succession paths $<y, s_\beta(y), ..., \mathbf{end}>$ pass through x. Thus, $s_\perp(y) \le x \ne s_\perp(x)$. This contradicts the fact that, since x is in $q_\beta(y)$, we must have $s_\perp(x) \le s_\perp(y)$. $\square$

For instance, since x_{14} of Figure 6.2 is the only iteration exit in the subtask $U(x_{14})$, its skeleton $q_+(x_{14})$ contains x_{14}. Will the converse be true also? That is to say, given that the skeleton $q_+(x_{14})$ contains x_{14}, will x_{14} be the only iteration exit in the subtask $U(x_{14})$? We shall prove that the converse of the theorem is also valid, thus obtaining a sufficient and necessary condition for unique iteration exit in a subtask.

Theorem 6.5.5

Given a subtask $U(x)$, the process x is the only iteration exit if and only if it is in one of the skeletons $q_\alpha(x)$.

Proof: We need only prove the converse of Theorem 6.5.4. If x is in $q_\alpha(x)$, it must be in $B_\alpha(x)$. By Proposition 6.2.3, $q_{-\alpha}(x)$ is empty. In other words, x cannot be in $B_{-\alpha}(x)$, and must therefore be an iteration exit. Assume that there is another iteration exit y. Since $q_{-\alpha}(x)$ is empty, y must also be in $B_\alpha(x)$. There are two possibilities.

(a) y is in $q_\alpha(x)$. Since x is also in $q_\alpha(x)$, $s_\perp(x) \ne s_\perp(y)$. This contradicts the fact that $U(x) = U(y)$ for iteration exits.

(b) y is not in $q_\alpha(x)$. Then there exists a process w $(\ne x)$ in $q_\alpha(x)$ such that y is in $U(w)$. Since x is in $q_\alpha(x)$, $s_\perp(w) \ne s_\perp(x)$. Hence $s_\perp(y) \le s_\perp(w) \ne s_\perp(x)$. This again contradicts the fact that $U(x) = U(y)$ for iteration exits. $\square$

We can therefore arrive at the following corollaries, which give sufficient and necessary conditions for a subtask to have no exit or multiple iteration exits.

Corollary 6.5.6

A subtask $U(x)$ has no exit if and only if x is a fork in one of the skeletons $q_\alpha(x)$.

Corollary 6.5.7

A subtask $U(x)$ has multiple iteration exits if and only if the process x is in one of the branches $B_\alpha(x)$ but not the corresponding skeleton $q_\alpha(x)$.

For example, since x_1 of Figure 6.2 is in the branch $B_+(x_1)$ but not the corresponding skeleton $q_+(x_1)$, the subtask $U(x_1)$ must have multiple iteration exits.

6.6 PARTIALLY OVERLAPPING SKELETONS

A skeleton $q_\beta(y)$ is said to be *fully embedded* in another skeleton $q_\alpha(x)$ if and only if y is a decision in $q_\alpha(x)$ and all the non-trivial processes in $q_\beta(y)$ are in $q_\alpha(x)$. Two skeletons $q_\alpha(x)$ and $q_\beta(y)$ are said to be *partially overlapping* if and only if neither one is fully embedded in the other but they contain some common non-trivial process $\neq x$ and y. For example, the following groups of skeletons in Figure 6.2 are partially overlapping:

(a) $q_+(\text{begin}) = <x_0, x_1, x_6, x_7, x_{17}>$
$q_+(x_3) = <x_4, x_0, x_1>$

(b) $q_-(x_7) = <x_{11}, x_{12}, x_{13}, x_{14}, x_{16}>$
$q_+(x_9) = <x_{13}, x_{14}, x_{16}>$
$q_+(x_{14}) = <x_{15}, x_{11}, x_{12}, x_{13}, x_{14}>$

These two groups of partially overlapping skeletons also happen to be connected with unstructuredness. Is this true in general? It will be the main task of investigation in the present section.

Lemma 6.6.1

Given a decision y, its skeleton $q_\beta(y)$ is fully embedded in another skeleton $q_\alpha(x)$ if and only if:

(a) y is a decision in $q_\alpha(x)$, and

(b) there exist a non-trivial process w in $q_\alpha(x)$ and a sequence of joins $<t_0, ..., t_n>$ in $q_\beta(y)$ such that

$$t_0 = s_\beta(y)$$
$$t_i = s_\perp(t_{i-1}) \text{ for } i = 1, ..., n \text{ (if } w \neq s_\perp(t_0))$$
$$w = s_\perp(t_n)$$

Proof: If $q_\beta(y)$ is fully embedded in $q_\alpha(x)$, then of course the conditions (a) and (b) above will be satisfied. Conversely, suppose the conditions (a) and (b) are satisfied. Since w is in $q_\alpha(x)$, there exists a sequence of processes $<v_0, ..., v_n>$ such that

$$v_0 = s_\alpha(x)$$
$$v_i = s_\perp(v_{i-1}) \text{ for } i = 1, ..., n \text{ (if } w \neq s_\alpha(x))$$
$$v_n = w$$

For any non-trivial process u in $q_\beta(y)$, there exists a sequence of processes $<v_n, ..., v_m>$ such that

$$v_n = w$$
$$v_i = s_\perp(v_{i-1}) \text{ for } i = n+1, ..., m \text{ (if } w \neq u)$$
$$v_m = u$$

Furthermore, $u \leq s_\perp(y) \leq s_\perp(x)$. Hence any non-trivial process u in $q_\beta(y)$ must lie in $q_\alpha(x)$. $\square$

Lemma 6.6.2

If $q_\alpha(x)$ and $q_\beta(y)$ are two partially overlapping skeletons, then:

(a) y is not a decision in $q_\alpha(x)$, or

(b) there exists a non-trivial process w in $q_\beta(y)$ but outside $q_\alpha(x)$ such that

$$t_0 = s_\beta(y)$$
$$t_i = s_\perp(t_{i-1}) \text{ for } i = 1, ..., n \text{ (if } w \neq s_\perp(t_0))$$
$$w = s_\perp(t_n)$$

for some joins $t_0, ..., t_n$ in $q_\beta(y)$.

Proof: The proof follows immediately from Lemma 6.6.1. $\square$

We can now derive the main theorems of this section, thus connecting unstructuredness in tasks with partially overlapping skeletons.

Theorem 6.6.3

A connected task is unstructured if there exist partially overlapping skeletons.

Proof: Given a connected task, suppose there exist partially overlapping skeletons $q_\alpha(x)$ and $q_\beta(y)$. By Lemma 6.6.2, we have two possibilities:

(a) y is not a decision in $q_\alpha(x)$. Suppose $U(y)$ is an iterative subtask. If y is a fork and there is no other exit, then $U(y)$ has no exit. If y is a decision, since there exists an elementary path from w to **end** not passing through y, by Lemma 6.5.1, there must be another exit. On the other hand, suppose $U(y)$ is a non-iterative subtask. Since there exists an elementary path from $x \notin U(y)$ to $w \in U(y)$ not passing through y, by definition, we must have an entry in the middle of a selection or parallel connection. Hence we have unstructuredness in either case.

(b) y is a decision in $q_\alpha(x)$ and there exists a non-trivial process w in $q_\beta(y)$ but outside $q_\alpha(x)$ such that

$$t_0 = s_\beta(y)$$
$$t_i = s_\perp(t_{i-1}) \text{ for } i = 1, ..., n \text{ (if } w \neq s_\perp(t_0))$$
$$w = s_\perp(t_n)$$

for some joins $t_0, ..., t_n$ in $q_\beta(y)$. Then w is an entry of $U(y)$. Since y is in $q_\alpha(x)$ and w is outside $q_\alpha(x)$, $y \neq w$. Hence w must be an entry in the middle of an iteration, selection or parallel connection. The task must therefore be unstructured. $\square$

We shall show that the converse of the theorem is also true, resulting in a necessary and sufficient condition for unstructuredness in tasks.

Theorem 6.6.4
A connected task is unstructured if and only if there exist partially overlapping skeletons.

Proof: We need only prove the converse of Theorem 6.6.3. Suppose a connected task is unstructured. By definition, there are four possible anomalies:

(a) *An Entry in the Middle of a Selection or Parallel Connection:* Let y ($\neq x$) be an entry in the middle of a non-iterative subtask $U(x)$. By Proposition 6.4.1, there exists a process w outside $U(x)$ such that one of its skeletons $q_\delta(w)$ contains y. We have two cases:

(i) y is in $q_\alpha(x)$. Since $U(x)$ is a non-iterative subtask, x is not in $q_\alpha(x)$. We therefore have two partially overlapping skeletons $q_\alpha(x)$ and $q_\delta(w)$ with a common non-trivial process y.

(ii) y is in $B_\alpha(x)$ but not in $q_\alpha(x)$. By Proposition 6.3.2, there exists a finite sequence of distinct skeletons $<q_{\varepsilon_0}(v_0), ..., q_{\varepsilon_n}(v_n)>$ such that

$$y \in q_{\varepsilon_0}(v_0)$$
$$v_{i-1} \in q_{\varepsilon_i}(v_i) \text{ for } i = 1, ..., n$$
$$v_n = x$$
$$\varepsilon_n = \alpha$$

Assume that there are no partially overlapping skeletons. Then $q_\delta(w)$ must contain v_0 also. By similar arguments, $q_\delta(w)$ must contain $v_1, ..., v_{n-1}$. Since $U(x)$ is a non-iterative subtask, x is not in $q_\alpha(x)$. In other words, v_n is not in $q_{\varepsilon_n}(v_n)$. Hence we have two partially overlapping skeletons $q_\delta(w)$ and $q_{\varepsilon_n}(v_n)$ with a common non-trivial process v_{n-1}.

(b) *Non-Unique Exit in an Iteration:* Let $U(x)$ be the iterative subtask and suppose that there exist non-unique exits. Let y be an entry of $U(x)$. We have three cases:

(i) There is no exit. Then x is a fork and, by Theorem 6.5.4, it is in one of the skeletons $q_\alpha(x)$. Furthermore, there exists a process w outside $U(x)$ such that one of its skeletons $q_\delta(w)$ contains x. Hence there exist two partially overlapping skeletons $q_\alpha(x)$ and $q_\delta(w)$ with a common fork x.

(ii) $y = x$ and there are multiple exits. Then there exists a process w outside $U(x)$ such that one of its skeletons $q_\delta(w)$ contains x. On the other hand, by Corollary 6.5.7, x is in neither of its own skeletons. Therefore there exists a process v ($\neq x$) in $U(x)$ such that one of its skeletons $q_\varepsilon(v)$ contains x. By the definition of skeletons, $s_\perp(x) \leq s_\perp(v)$. But since v ($\neq s_\perp(x)$) is in $U(x)$, $s_\perp(v) \leq s_\perp(x)$. Hence $s_\perp(v) = s_\perp(x)$, so that v and x cannot both be in $q_\delta(w)$. In other words, there exist partially overlapping skeletons $q_\delta(w)$ and $q_\varepsilon(v)$ with a common non-trivial process x.

(iii) $y \neq x$ and there are multiple exits. Then there exists a process w outside $U(x)$ such that one of its skeletons $q_\delta(w)$ contains y. If $q_\delta(w)$ does not contain x, then $q_\alpha(x)$ and $q_\delta(w)$ are partially overlapping skeletons with a common non-trivial process y. If $q_\delta(w)$ contains x, then, by arguments similar to (ii), there exist partially overlapping skeletons $q_\delta(w)$ and $q_\varepsilon(v)$ with a common non-trivial process x.

(c) *An Entry in the Middle of an Iteration:* Let y be an entry in the middle of an iterative subtask $U(x)$. By Proposition 6.4.1, there exists a process w outside $U(x)$ such that one of its skeletons $q_\delta(w)$ contains y. We have four cases:

(i) $y = x$. In this case, there exists another entry v ($\neq x$) in $q_\alpha(x)$. Assume that there are no partially overlapping skeletons. Then v must also be in $q_\delta(w)$. Since $v \leq x$, $q_\delta(w)$ must be of the form $<..., v, ..., x, ...>$, which contradicts the fact that $y = x$ is an entry.

(ii) y ($\neq x$) is in $q_\alpha(x)$ and there exists another entry y' ($\neq x$) in $U(x)$. By Proposition 6.4.1, there exists another process w' outside $U(x)$ such that one of its skeletons $q_{\delta'}(w')$ contains y'. By Proposition 6.3.1, there exists a finite sequence of distinct skeletons $<q_{\varepsilon_0}(v_0), ..., q_{\varepsilon_n}(v_n)>$ such that

$$y' \in q_{\varepsilon_0}(v_0)$$
$$v_{i-1} \in q_{\varepsilon_i}(v_i) \text{ for } i = 1, ..., n \text{ (if } y' \notin q_\alpha(x) \text{ and } q_{-\alpha}(x))$$
$$v_n = x$$

Assume that there are no partially overlapping skeletons. Then $q_\delta(w)$ must be of the form $<..., y, ..., x, ...>$. On the other hand, $q_{\varepsilon_0}(v_0)$ should be fully embedded in $q_{\delta'}(w')$, so that v_0 must be in $q_{\delta'}(w')$. By similarly arguments, $v_1, ..., v_{n-1}$ and x are also in $q_{\delta'}(w')$. Hence $q_{\delta'}(w')$ must be of the form $<..., y', ..., v_0, ..., v_{n-1}, ..., x, ...>$. Since both the selections $q_\delta(w)$ and $q_{\delta'}(w')$ contain x, one of them should be fully embedded in the other. Without loss of generality, suppose $q_{\delta'}(w')$ is fully embedded in $q_\delta(w)$. Then $q_\delta(w)$ is of the form $<..., y, ..., w', ..., y', ..., x, ...>$. As a result, w' would be in $q_\alpha(x)$, contradicting the fact that w' is outside $U(x)$.

(iii) y ($\neq x$) is in $q_\alpha(x)$ but there is no other entry in $U(x)$. In this case, y is not a normal entry. Since $y \neq x$, there exists a non-trivial process y' in $q_\alpha(x)$ such that either $y = s_\perp(y')$ or, for some joins $t_0, \ldots, t_n$ in $U(x)$,

$$t_0 = s_\perp(y')$$
$$t_i = s_\perp(t_{i-1}) \text{ for } i = 1, \ldots, n \text{ (if } y \neq s_\perp(t_0))$$
$$y = s_\perp(t_n)$$

Assume that there are no partially overlapping skeletons. Then both y and y' are in $q_\delta(w)$. Hence $q_\delta(w)$ is of the form $<\ldots, y', \ldots, y, \ldots>$, which contradicts the fact that y is an entry.

(iv) y ($\neq x$) is not in $q_\alpha(x)$. Assume that there are no partially overlapping skeletons. Then y is in $q_\varepsilon(v)$ for some process v ($\neq x$) in $U(x)$. By arguments similar to (ii) above, $q_\delta(w)$ must be of the form $<\ldots, y, \ldots, v, \ldots, x, \ldots>$. Since y is not in $q_\alpha(x)$, we must have two partially overlapping skeletons $q_\alpha(x)$ and $q_\delta(w)$ with a common non-trivial process y.

(d) *An Exit in the Middle of a Selection or Parallel Connection:* Suppose that the branches $B_\alpha(x)$ and $B_{-\alpha}(x)$ have some non-trivial process in common. By definition, there exist a process w in $B_\alpha(x)$ but outside $B_{-\alpha}(x)$, and another process v in $B_{-\alpha}(x)$ but outside $B_\alpha(x)$, such that their skeletons $q_\delta(w)$ and $q_\varepsilon(v)$ are partially overlapping. $\square$

A straightforward corollary to our main theorem is that a connected task will be structured if and only there are no partially overlapping skeletons.

6.7 CONCLUSION

In this chapter, we introduced the concepts of elementary succession paths, least common successors, skeletons and minimal subtasks. We defined unstructuredness in terms of these concepts. We also introduced the notions of fully embedded skeletons and partially overlapping skeletons. We showed that only one single criterion would be necessary and sufficient for the identification of unstructured tasks. Namely, a connected task is unstructured if and only if there exist partially overlapping skeletons. As a straightforward corollary, we can also conclude that the absence of partially overlapping skeletons is necessary and sufficient for proving a task to be structured. The theorems are also useful for proving the structuredness of programs in general.

7 A Prototype System to Implement the Unifying Framework

All this will not be finished in the first one hundred days. Nor will it be finished in the first one thousand days, ... But let us begin.

—*John F. Kennedy* (1961)

7.1 INTRODUCTION

In this chapter, we shall give an illustration of the practical usefulness of our framework. We shall discuss a prototype system which has been developed to implement the structured tasks. It has been implemented on a Macintosh using Turbo Pascal. It enables the user to draw a hierarchy of DeMarco-like task diagrams and stores them as structured tasks, which are stored physically in the form of pointers and linked lists. It helps the user to review the task diagrams to an appropriate level of detail, and zoom in/zoom out to lower/higher levels through refinements and abstractions as required. Given an incomplete task specification, the system prompts the user to define further details of his design considerations. For example, if the user wants to build a hierarchical structure into a flat task diagram, he will be prompted to supply the necessary details such as the names of intermediate levels. Given a hierarchy of task diagrams, the system then transforms them automatically into a term algebra, a Yourdon structure chart and also Jackson structure text. An example of an application of the system will be given in Section 7.2. An overview of the system with examples of its algorithms will be given in Section 7.3.

7.2 EXAMPLE ON AN APPLICATION OF THE SYSTEM

We would like to explain the functions of the system by working through an example. Sample outputs of the system are given in Figures 7.1 to 7.24.

The system consists of two programs. The first program (see Figure 7.1) captures a DeMarco-like task diagram and stores it as a task structure file and a event structure file. The second program (see Figure 7.14) reads the two files thus captured and transforms the the task structure into a term algebra, a Yourdon structure chart and also Jackson structure text. Both of these programs interact with the user through windows, mouse pointers and pull-down menus.

(a) *Creating the top window of a DeMarco-like task diagram:* Consider the example we have used in Chapters 4 and 5. Suppose we wish to draw a task diagram with a multi-level structure, as in Figure 4.5. Each level will be shown on the screen as one window. The contents of different windows will be drawn in different colours if the system is run on a Macintosh II with a colour monitor. They will appear in black and white if run on a Macintosh SE or Macintosh Plus.

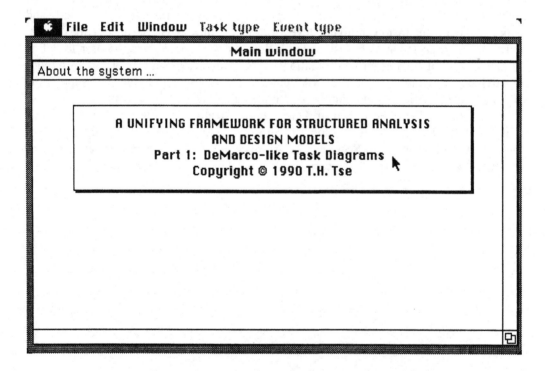

Figure 7.1 Program to Create DeMarco-like Task Diagrams

Let us first of all draw the top window. This is illustrated in Figure 7.2. The system will prompt the user to click the location of the root bubble and to specify its name. After creating the root bubble, the user should click the Event Type menu to specify whether the input/output events for the bubble are pure data, flags, files, sources or sinks. A sample Event Type menu is shown at the top of Figure 7.2. The user should also specify the names of the input/output events. A root bubble will then be drawn.

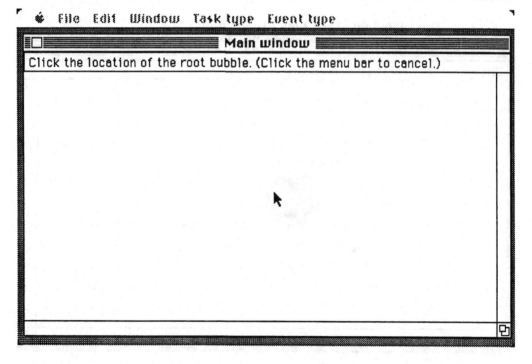

Figure 7.2 Creating the Top Window of a DeMarco-like Task Diagram

(b) *Zooming into a child window:* The user will of course want to specify more details than just the root bubble. He can do so by selecting the "to child" option in the Window menu (see the top of Figure 7.3), meaning that he wants to zoom into the window of one of the bubbles. He will be prompted to select the appropriate bubble, as shown in Figure 7.3. A new window will pop up, as in Figure 7.4. Since the window currently contains no bubble, the user is asked to specify the location of the first bubble. Similarly to the root bubble, the user is also asked to supply the name of the bubble, select the type of the input/output events, and specify their names. If the user wants to add a second or more bubbles after the first one, it can be done through the "insert" option in the Edit menu (see the top of Figure 7.5). The system then prompts the user to locate the bubble, enter its name and specify the type and name of the input/output events.

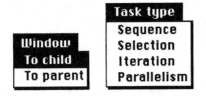

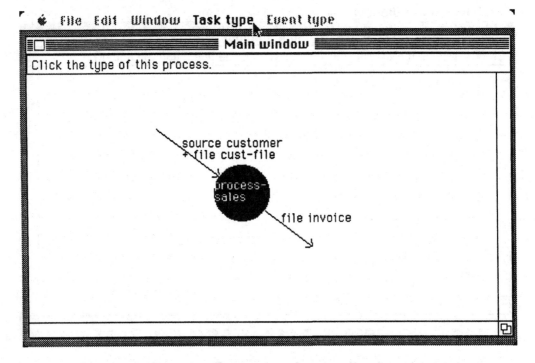

Figure 7.3 Zooming Into a Child Window

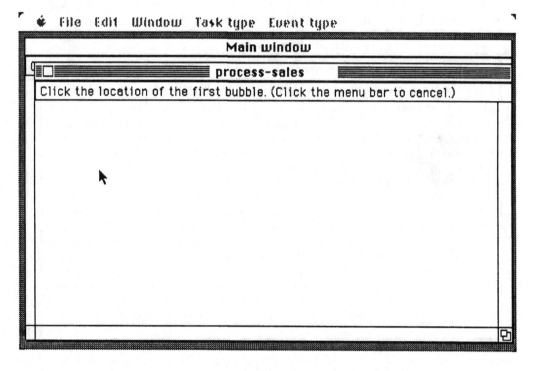

Figure 7.4 Creating a Bubble in a Child Window

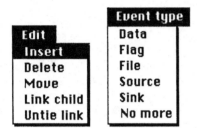

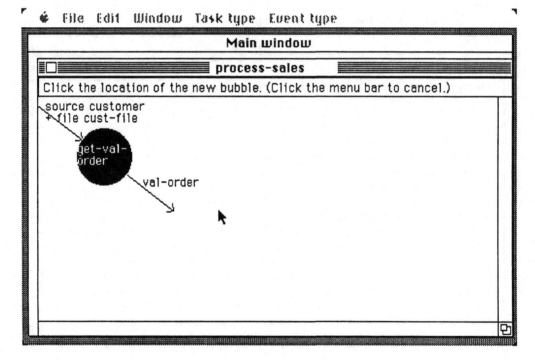

Figure 7.5 Inserting Further Bubbles in a Window

This is continued until all the required bubbles have been specified. The final outcome is shown in Figure 7.6.

(c) *Zooming further down a child window:* We may want to zoom into more details for each bubble in the second level of the task diagrams. This may be continued using the "to child" option as illustrated in Figure 7.6, so that a further window is drawn up as in Figure 7.7.

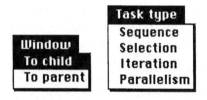

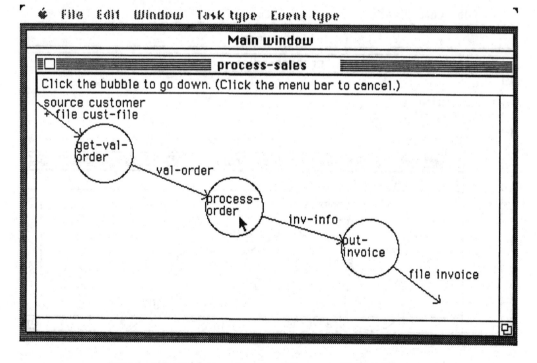

Figure 7.6 Zooming Further Down a Child Window

(*d*) *Moving a window to a desired location:* Very often, when we have quite a
number of windows drawn on the screen, the spacing may not be according to the
wishes of the user. We can move a window to a new location by clicking the
"drag bar" at the top of the window and dragging it to a new location, as in
Figure 7.7. The result is shown in Figure 7.8.

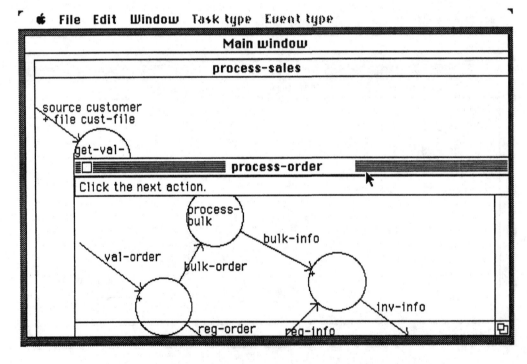

Figure 7.7 Moving a Window to a Desired Location

(*e*) *Changing the size of a window:* Although the window has been moved to a more
desirable position, the window may still be too small to accommodate all the
bubbles. We can click on the "grow" box in the bottom right hand corner of the
window and drag it so that the window will grow to a more reasonable size. For
example, after dragging the grow box of the window of Figure 7.8, an enlarged
window as in Figure 7.9 will result.

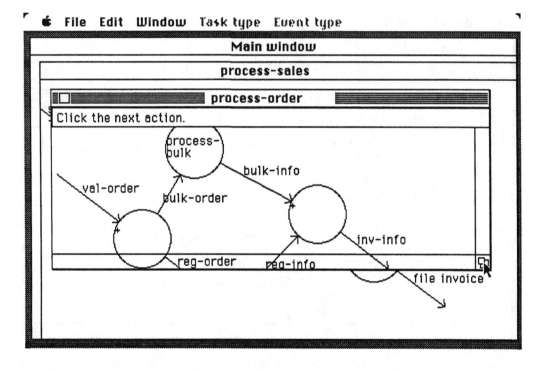

Figure 7.8 Changing the Size of a Window

(f) *Zooming out of a child window:* Some users may not want to see all the details
   in a certain window. We can forget about the detailed window and zoom out to
   an upper level by clicking the "go away" box in the upper left hand corner of the
   window. For instance, if we click the box in Figure 7.9, we shall end up with the
   situation in Figure 7.10. Alternatively, we can also use the "to parent" option in
   the Window menu, shown at the top of Figure 7.9. The outcome will be exactly
   the same.

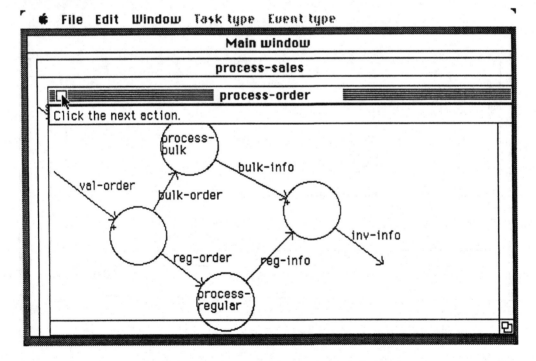

Figure 7.9 Zooming Out of a Child Window

(g) *Linking up the bubbles of a child window with those of the current window:*
Sometimes we may not want the task diagrams to appear in too many levels. We
may want our specification to appear in a flat form as in Figure 4.6. This may be
done through a "link child" option in the Edit menu. The bubbles in a child
window will then be linked to the bubbles in the parent window. For example, if
we click "process-order" in Figure 7.10, then this bubble in the parent window
will be replaced by all the bubbles in Figure 7.9, thus resulting in Figure 7.11.

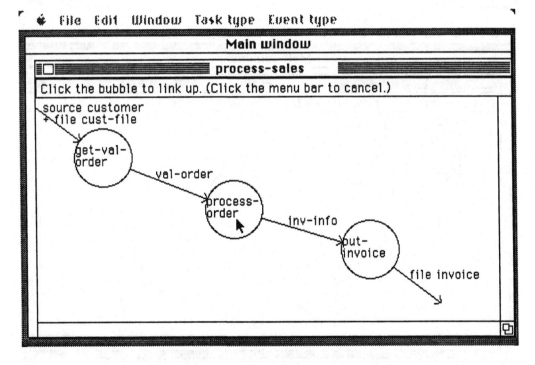

**Figure 7.10 Linking up the Bubbles of a Child Window
with those of the Current Window**

(h) *Moving a bubble to a desired location:* After linking up two or more windows, the bubbles may crumble against one another. By using the "move" option in the Edit menu, as shown in Figure 7.11, the bubbles can be relocated according to the wishes of the user. The result will be like Figure 7.12.

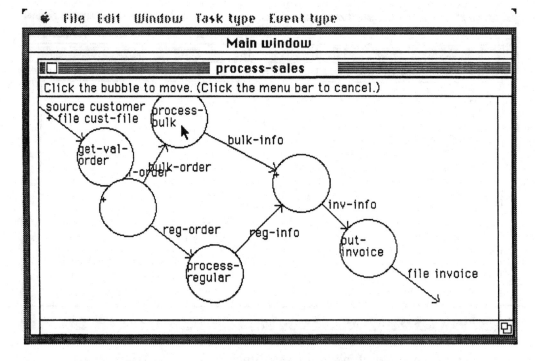

Figure 7.11 Moving a Bubble to a Desired Location

(*i*) *Separating the bubbles of a child window from its parent window:* If we do not want a flat task diagram, the bubbles in a child window may be "untied" from its parent window, as shown in Figure 7.12. We shall then be back to the parent window as in Figure 7.13.

(*j*) *Deleting a bubble from a window:* Sometimes one or more of the bubbles may no longer be required. They may be removed using the "delete" option of the Edit menu. The system will prompt the user to click the bubble to be removed, as shown in Figure 7.13.

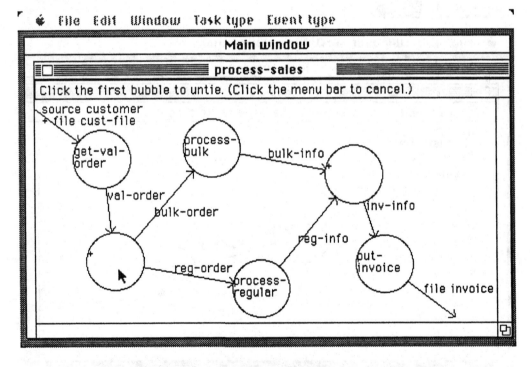

**Figure 7.12 Separating the Bubbles of a Child Window
from its Parent Window**

(k) *Saving a DeMarco-like task diagram:* We have seen that we can manipulate a task diagram by creating new bubbles, deleting useless ones, zooming in or zooming out of windows, and moving the location of windows or bubbles when necessary. A multi-level DeMarco-like task diagram will result. It is stored in the system as structured tasks or, in physical terms, pointers and linked lists. But users will not be required to be acquainted with these physical concepts. If any information is required in order to prepare the structured task, the system will ask the user to respond to its prompts.

When we are satisfied with the task diagram, we can select the "quit" option of the File menu, shown at the top of Figure 7.13. The task structure will be saved

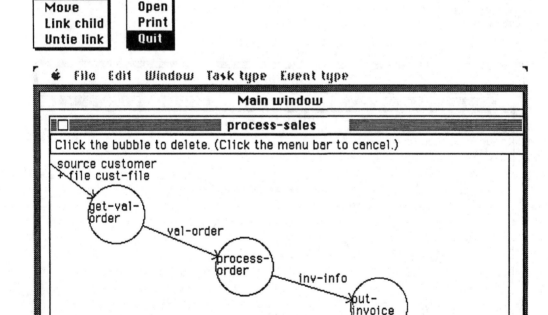

Figure 7.13 Deleting a Bubble from a Window

automatically in a file known as "outTask", and the event structure will be saved in "outEvent". If we want to return to the saved states in some other occasion, we can call the program again and open the files by selecting the "open" option in the File menu.

(*l*) *Transforming DeMarco-like task diagrams into other structured models:* To transform the structured tasks into other structured models, the *Transform* program highlighted in Figure 7.14 will be required. Mapping the tasks into a term algebra or Jackson structure text will be straightforward and automatic, as shown in Figures 7.15 and 7.16. Mapping the tasks into a Yourdon structure chart is shown in Figures 7.17 to 7.24.

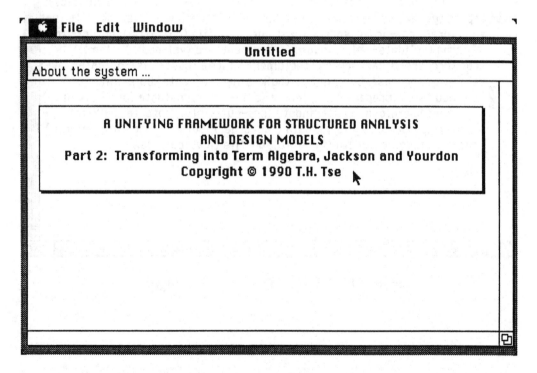

Figure 7.14 Program to Transform DeMarco-like Task Diagrams into other Structured Models

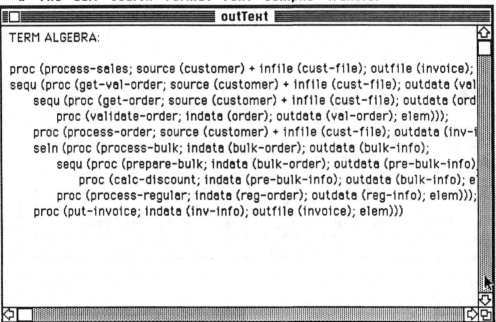

Figure 7.15 Transforming into Term Algebra

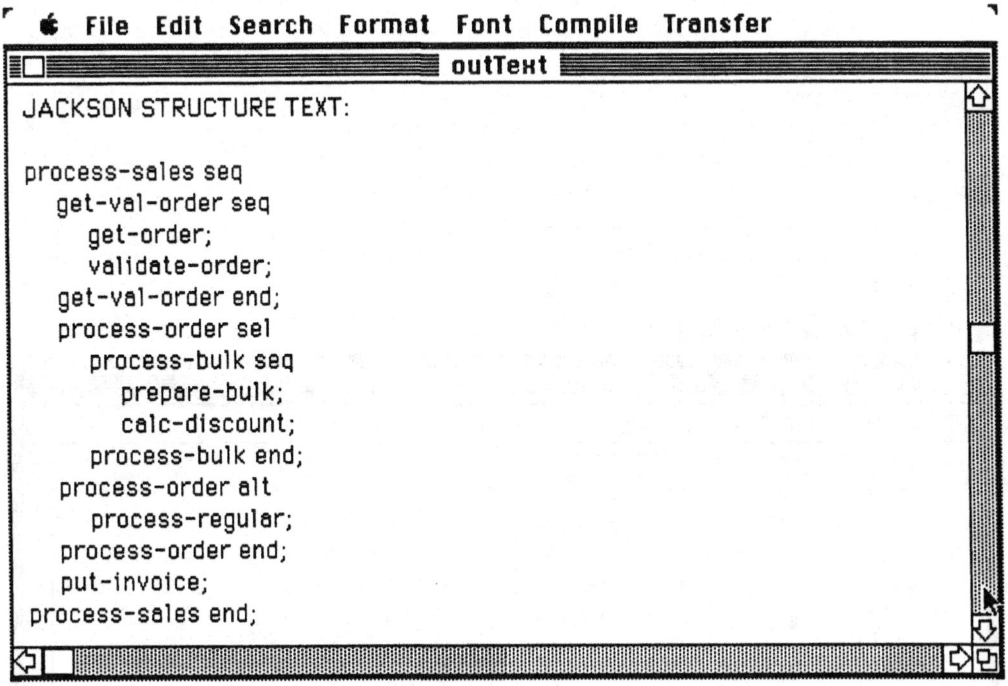

```
 ╔═══════════════════════════════════════════════════════════════════════╗
    🍎  File   Edit   Search   Format   Font   Compile   Transfer
 ╠═══════════════════════════════════════════════ outText ═══════════════╣
 │ JACKSON STRUCTURE TEXT:                                              ⬆ │
 │                                                                        │
 │ process-sales seq                                                      │
 │    get-val-order seq                                                   │
 │       get-order;                                                       │
 │       validate-order;                                                  │
 │    get-val-order end;                                                  │
 │    process-order sel                                                   │
 │       process-bulk seq                                                 │
 │          prepare-bulk;                                                 │
 │          calc-discount;                                                │
 │       process-bulk end;                                                │
 │    process-order alt                                                   │
 │       process-regular;                                                 │
 │    process-order end;                                                  │
 │    put-invoice;                                                        │
 │ process-sales end;                                                  ⬇ │
 ╚════════════════════════════════════════════════════════════════════════╝
```

Figure 7.16 Transforming into Jackson Structure Text

(*m*) *Transforming into Yourdon structure chart:* For each of the boxes in the Yourdon structure chart, the user is prompted to specify its location, as in Figure 7.17,
so that the chart can be draw up according to the user's wishes. A window in the
DeMarco program will correspond to a window in this program, which contains
one level of a structure chart, as we can see in Figure 7.18. A user may want to
zoom into the details of a certain box in the structure chart. This may be done
through the "to child" option of the Window menu. An example is given in
Figure 7.18. A new window will appear as a result. If the system has already
acquired the locations of the boxes in the child window, then the boxes will be
displayed automatically. Otherwise the user will be prompted to select the location of each box. The final outcome is shown in Figure 7.19.

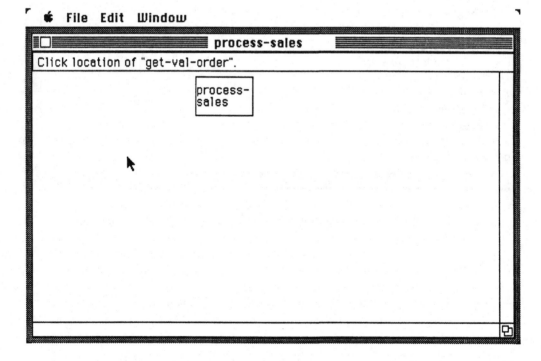

Figure 7.17 Specifying the Locations of Boxes in Yourdon Structure Chart

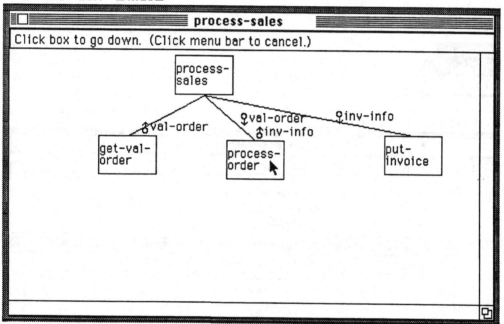

Figure 7.18 Zooming Into a Child Window

(n) *Manipulation of Yourdon structure chart:* Moving or enlarging of windows may be done as usual. We can zoom further down a child window by using the "to child" option of the Window menu shown in Figure 7.19. In this case, Figure 7.20 will result. As in the *DeMarco* program, zooming out of a child window can be effected through either the "to parent" option of the Window menu, or the "go away" box of the window, as in Figure 7.20.

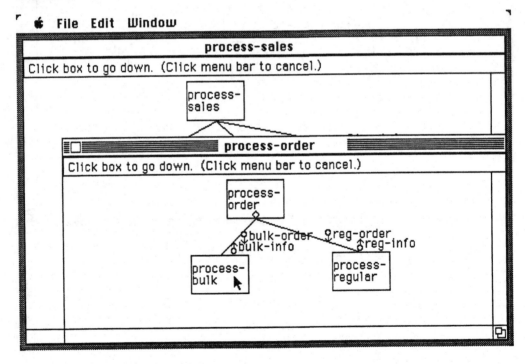

Figure 7.19 Zooming Further Down a Child Window

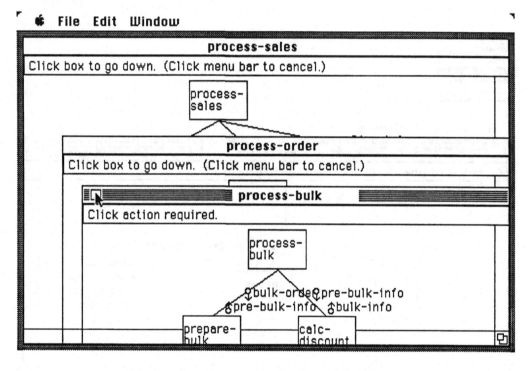

Figure 7.20 Zooming Out of a Child Window

(o) *Linking up the boxes of a child window with those of the current window:* Since Yourdon structure charts are much more condensed in size than task diagrams, we do not need too many levels of windows to accommodate the boxes. More often, we want several levels in a structure chart to be grouped together in the same window. This can be achieved by using the "link child" option of the Edit menu (see Figure 7.21). The result is shown in Figure 7.22.

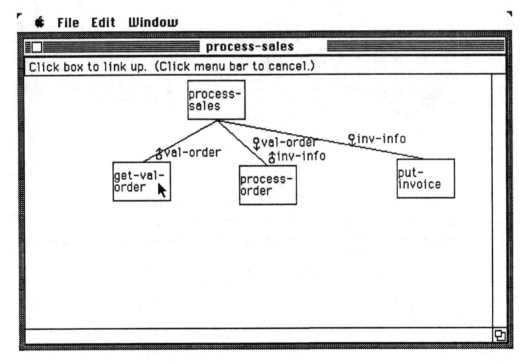

**Figure 7.21 Linking up the Boxes of a Child Window
with those of the Current Window**

(*p*) *Moving a box to a desired location:* The spacing of the boxes in a first draft may look awkward, as we can see in Figure 7.22. We can move the bubbles using the "move" option in the Edit menu, resulting in Figure 7.23.

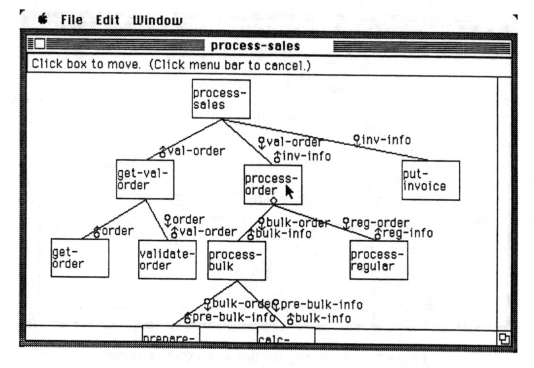

Figure 7.22 **Moving a Box to a Desired Location**

(q) *Separating the boxes of a child window from those of the parent window:* Finally, the "untie" option is also available for structure charts. If we untie the group of boxes under "process-order" in Figure 7.23, for instance, we will get Figure 7.24.

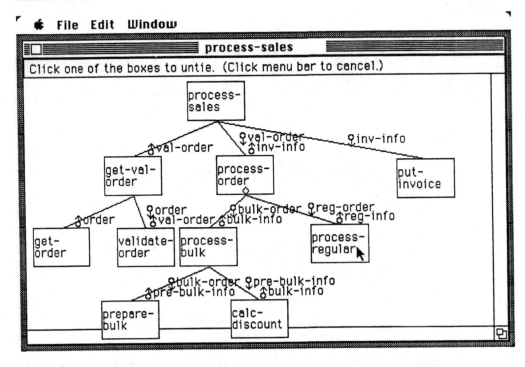

**Figure 7.23 Separating the Boxes of a Child Window
from those of the Parent Window**

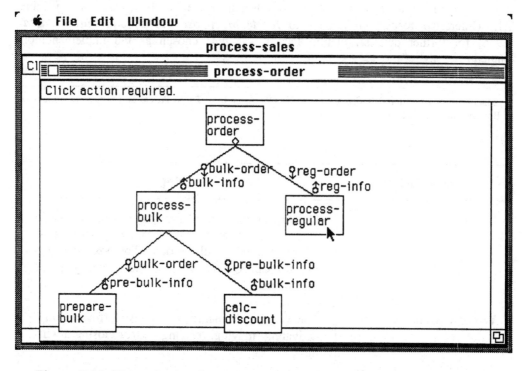

Figure 7.24 Example showing a Second Level Window which is Separated from the Top Level but Linked to the Boxes in a Third Level Window

7.3 SYSTEM CHARACTERISTICS

In this section, we shall give further details of the prototype system for implementing the unifying framework of structured models. Readers not interested in program implementation details may skip the rest of the chapter.

7.3.1 Choice of Development Language

It was considered appropriate for the prototype system to be run on a reasonably priced computer system with menu-driven interactive graphics. A Macintosh[®] was chosen because it is a popular personal computer environment with a user-friendly operating system which supports window graphics, mouse pointers and pull-down menus. Furthermore, the software development for such graphics, menus and mouse operations can be handled easily by Turbo Pascal[®] using Macintosh QuickDraw and other software managers in the Macintosh User-Interface Toolbox, as shown in Table 7.1. (Interested readers may refer to *Inside Macintosh* (1985) and *Turbo Pascal* (1986) for further details.) Turbo Pascal was thus chosen as the implementation language.

[®] Macintosh is a registered trademark of Apple Computer Inc. Turbo Pascal is a registered trademark of Borland International Inc.

Toolbox Facility	Description
QuickDraw	QuickDraw handles all the graphics operations in Macintosh. It can be called easily by Turbo Pascal. Furthermore, all the other Toolbox Managers in turn call QuickDraw for their own graphics operations.
Window Manager	The Window Manager is responsible for creating, activating, moving, resizing and/or closing a window.
Menu Manager	The Menu Manager helps us to display menus for the user to pick his choice. It also passes on the user's choice to the application program for action.

**Table 7.1 Software Managers in the Macintosh User-Interface Toolbox
(Part 1 of 2)**

Toolbox Facility	Description
Resource Manager	The Resource Manager allows us to separate menus from the source code of an application program so that the updating of menus can be done by a user who is not familiar with the source code.
Toolbox Event Manager	The Toolbox Event Manager reports to the application program when the user clicks the mouse or strikes a key. It also reports on any occurrence within an application program which requires a response. For example, when a window which was partially hidden becomes fully exposed, the application program will be told to redraw it.
Font Manager	If the graphics contain text, the Font Manager helps to select the font types and sizes of the messages displayed.
Dialogue Manager	The Dialogue Manager helps to alert the user by displaying error messages on the screen and asking for possible actions to be selected.
Control Manager	The Control Manager is responsible for special controls within a window, such as check boxes and scroll bars. If such controls have been clicked by the user, the Control Manager will inform the application program accordingly.
Desk Manager	The Desk Manager enables the user to call the Macintosh control panel or other desk accessories (such as calculators) while he is running an application program.

Table 7.1 Software Managers in the Macintosh User Interface Toolbox
(Part 2 of 2)

7.3.2 Components of the Prototype System
The system consists of two programs:

(a) *DeMarco Program:* The *DeMarco* program prompts the user to draw a multi-level DeMarco-like task diagram and, at the same time, captures the task structure using pointers and linked lists. It is a 48 kbyte program written in Turbo Pascal and contains about 2200 lines of source code. The program will display windows in different colours if it is run on a Macintosh II with a colour monitor. Otherwise if it is run on a Macintosh SE or a Macintosh Plus, windows will appear in black and white. The modules making up the program are listed in Table 7.2.

Subprogram	Description
addBubble	Insert a new bubble to a window.
bubbleTo	Draw a bubble for the current process and draw a line linking it to the previous bubble.
copyRight	Show a copyright box.
cutBubble	Delete a bubble from a window.
downBubble	Open a child window for the bubble picked by the user.
drawEventName	Display the name of a event with the necessary syntax editing.
drawProcName	Display the name of a process with the necessary syntax editing.
drawSubBubbles	Draw the child bubbles of a specified process.
drawWindows	Redraw all the windows of a multi-level task diagram.
errorAtTop	Function to check whether the specified action is appropriate for an empty and/or top window.
findOwner	Recursive subprogram within ownerOf.
firstOf	Function to find the first child bubble of a given process.

Table 7.2 Subprograms of the *DeMarco* Program
(Part 1 of 3)

Subprogram	Description
getFileName	Display a dialogue box and prompt the user to specify the name of the input file.
getEventInfo	Display a dialogue box and prompt the user to specify the details of the input/output event.
getProcName	Display a dialogue box and prompt the user to specify the name of a process.
handleMenu	Accept the user's choice in the menu.
initBubble	Set the initial values of a bubble.
initToolbox	Initialize the Macintosh Toolbox.
keyControl	Handle control keys.
lastOf	Function to find the last child bubble of a given process.
linkBubbles	Link the current process to its child bubbles.
makeTasks	Prepare a DeMarco-like task diagram.
mouseControl	Handle an event caused by clicking or movement of the mouse.
moveBubble	Move a specified bubble to a new location.
newTasks	Create a new task structure.
openBubble	Create a new bubble.
ownerOf	Function to find the process which owns the current window.
pickAction	Prompt the user to pick an action.
pickBubble	Prompt the user to pick a bubble, and remember also the bubble prior to the one picked.
pickEventType	Prompt the user to pick the type of event.
pickProcType	Prompt the user to pick the type of process.
preSave	Initialize the conditions and values before saving the task structures in permanent files.

Table 7.2 Subprograms of the *DeMarco* Program
(Part 2 of 3)

Subprogram	Description
printPrompt	Prompt the user to dump the current screen on to a printer using standard Macintosh facilities.
prompt	Display a message to the user.
pushStack	Store the identity of the front window at the top of a stack.
readMouse	Find the location of the mouse pointer.
readName	Read the name of a process or event and do the necessary syntax editing.
readTasks	Read the task structure which was saved in a previous run of the *DeMarco* program.
reverseColour	Show the subsequent drawings as white lines on a coloured background, for the purpose of highlighting.
save	Save the task structure in permanent files.
searchBubble	Recursive subprogram within pickBubble. It searches through all the bubbles under a specified process for the one which has been picked by the user.
serialOf	Function to find the serial number of first child.
setColour	Set the colour of the drawings in the current window. If the colour has been reversed (see reverseColour above), then reset it to normal.
shapeWindow	Change the size of a window.
shutWindow	Close a window.
untieBubbles	Do not show the picked bubbles in the current window but push them down to a child window.
updateWindow	Update the current window according to the mouse or control keys.
windowFound	Function to check whether a specified window has already been drawn on the screen.
writeName	Write the name of a process or event in a permanent file with the necessary syntax editing.

Table 7.2 Subprograms of the *DeMarco* Program (Part 3 of 3)

(b) *Transform Program:* The *Transform* program maps the structured task thus captured into a term in the initial algebra, a hierarchy of Yourdon structure charts and lines of Jackson structure text. It is a 54 kbyte program written in Turbo Pascal, and contains about 1800 lines of source code. The program will display windows in different colours if it is run on a Macintosh II with a colour monitor. The modules making up the program are listed in Table 7.3.

Subprogram	Description
algebra	Transform a task structure into a term in the initial algebra.
boxTo	Draw a box for the current process and draw a line linking it to the parent box.
copyRight	Show a copyright box.
downBox	Open a child window for the box picked by the user.
drawEventName	Display the name of a event with the necessary syntax editing.
drawProcName	Display the name of a process with the necessary syntax editing.
drawSubTree	Draw a subtree in a Yourdon structure chart with the specified process as the root.
drawWindows	Redraw all the windows of the hierarchy of Yourdon structure charts.
errorAtTop	Function to check whether the specified action is appropriate for an empty and/or top window.
findOwner	Recursive subprogram within ownerOf.
firstOf	Function to find the first child of a given process.
getFileName	Display a dialogue box and prompt the user to specify the name of the input file.
handleMenu	Accept the user's choice in the menu.
initToolbox	Initialize the Macintosh Toolbox.
Jackson	Transform a task structure into Jackson structure text.

Table 7.3 Subprograms of the *Transform* Program
(Part 1 of 3)

Subprogram	Description
keyControl	Handle control keys.
lastOf	Function to find the last child of a given process.
linkBox	Link the current process to its child boxes.
mouseControl	Handle an event caused by clicking or movement of the mouse.
moveBox	Move a specified box to a new location.
openBox	Create a new box.
ownerOf	Function to find the process which owns the current window.
pickAction	Prompt the user to pick an action.
pickBox	Prompt the user to pick a box.
preAlgebra	Initialize the conditions and values before transforming the task structures into a term algebra.
printPrompt	Prompt the user to dump the current screen on to a printer using standard Macintosh facilities.
prompt	Display a message to the user.
pushStack	Store the identity of the front window at the top of a stack.
readMouse	Find the location of the mouse pointer.
readName	Read the name of a process or event and do the necessary syntax editing.
readTasks	Read the task structure saved in the *DeMarco* program.
reverseColour	Show the subsequent drawings as white lines on a coloured background, for the purpose of highlighting.
searchBox	Recursive subprogram within pickBox. It searches through all the box under a specified process for the one which has been picked by the user.
serialOf	Function to find the serial number allocated to a specified bubble.

Table 7.3 Subprograms of the *Transform* Program
(Part 2 of 3)

Subprogram	Description
setColour	Set the colour of the drawings in the current window. If the colour has been reversed (see reverseColour above), then reset it to normal.
shapeWindow	Change the size of a window.
shutWindow	Close a window.
smallBubble	Draw an input/output in the Yourdon structure chart.
untieBox	Do not show the picked boxes in the current window but push them down to a child window.
updateWindow	Update the current window according to the mouse or control keys.
windowFound	Function to check whether a specified window has already been drawn on the screen.
writeName	Write the name of a process or event in a permanent file with the necessary syntax editing.
Yourdon	Transform a task structure into layers of Yourdon structure charts.

Table 7.3 Subprograms of the *Transform* Program
(Part 3 of 3)

7.3.3 Examples of Algorithms

Let γ be a refinement mapping T into T'. Then for any standard process $<e, p, e'> \in T$, there exists a structured subtask $U(e, e') \subseteq T'$ such that

$$\gamma(\{<e, p, e'>\}) = U.$$

Since U is structured, we have two possibilities:

(a) If it is a sequence, there exists a standard process x whose input event $= e$.
(b) Otherwise there exists an auxiliary process y whose input event $= e$.

Given a standard process $<e, p, e'>$, therefore, we can link it with an initial process x or y in U. Furthermore, we can use pointers to join x or y with the rest of the processes in U by tracing the input/output events. Thus, given a parent process, it can be refined into the child processes through a pointer linked to the first child plus one or more chains linked to the other children. In this way, the concepts of task structures and refinements can be implemented by means of recursive subprograms which manipulate pointers and linked lists.

The algorithms for selected modules of the system are listed in Figures 7.25 to 7.30 in order to give readers an idea of the processing involved. Explanatory notes are found in *italics* in the figures. The algorithms listed include:

(*a*) Selecting a bubble in a DeMarco-like task diagram;
(*b*) Inserting a bubble into a task diagram;
(*c*) Deleting a bubble from a task diagram;
(*d*) Drawing a Yourdon structure chart;
(*e*) Transforming a task structure into a term in the initial algebra;
(*f*) Transforming a task structure into Jackson structure text.

procedure pickBubble (parent, picked, prior):
{*This is a procedure in the* DeMarco *program which prompts the user to pick a bubble shown under a* parent *window. It also remembers the bubble prior to the one picked.*}

subprocedure searchBubble (parent, picked, prior, point):
{*The main procedure contains a subprocedure* searchBubble, *which searches through all the bubbles under the* parent *process for the one which has been picked by the user.*}

{First of all, find the first child of the parent process:}
begin
process := firstOf (parent);
prior := **nil**;

{*Search the processes in the main path:*}
while picked = **nil and** process ≠ **nil do**
    with process↑ **do**

        {*If a process is linked to its own children, then continue to search downwards:*}
        begin
        if linkedToChild **then**
            searchBubble (process, picked, prior, point)

        {*Otherwise if the mouse points to the interior of a bubble, then the required*}

Figure 7.25 Algorithm for Selecting a Bubble
in the DeMarco-like Task Diagram
(Part 1 of 3)

{*Otherwise if the mouse points to the interior of a bubble, then the required process is found:*}
else if inBubble (point, process) **then**
    picked := process;

{*Otherwise continue to search the next child of the same parent:*}
if picked = **nil then**
    begin
    prior := process;
    process := nextProcess
    end
end;

{*If it is not found in the main path, than search the processes in the side path:*}
if picked = **nil and** parent ≠ **nil then**
    begin
    prior := firstOf (parent);
    process := prior↑.altProcess;
    while picked = **nil and** process ≠ **nil do**
        with process↑ **do**

        {*If a process is linked to its own children, then continue to search downwards:*}
        begin
        if linkedToChild **then**
            searchBubble (process, picked, prior, point)

        {*Otherwise if the mouse points to the interior of a bubble, then it is found:*}
        else if inBubble (point, process) **then**
            picked := process;

        {*Otherwise continue to search the next child of the same parent:*}
        if picked = **nil then**
            begin
            prior := process;
            process := nextProcess
            end
    end

**Figure 7.25 Algorithm for Selecting a Bubble
in the DeMarco-like Task Diagram
(Part 2 of 3)**

```
      end
   end;
   {End of the searchBubble subprocedure.}
```

{*The main procedure* pickBubble *starts here. First of all, prompt the user to pick a bubble:*}
```
begin
readMouse (point);
```

{*Call the subprocedure* searchBubble *to search all the bubbles under the parent for the one which has been picked by the user. If it cannot be found, prompt the user again and repeat the procedure until the user picks a right bubble or decides to quit by pointing to the menu bar:*}
```
if firstOf (parent) = lastOf (parent)
and not insertion then
    picked := firstOf (parent)
else
   begin
   picked := nil;
   while picked = nil
   and not inMenuBar (point) do
      begin
      searchBubble (parent, picked, prior, point);
      if picked = nil then
         readMouse (point)
      end
   end;
```

{*If the relevant bubble is found, then draw it in reversed colour:*}
```
if picked ≠ nil
   begin
   reverseColour (parent);
   openBubble (picked);
   setColour (parent)
   end
end;
```

**Figure 7.25 Algorithm for Selecting a Bubble
in the DeMarco-like Task Diagram
(Part 3 of 3)**

procedure addBubble (parent):
{*This is a procedure in the* DeMarco *program which prompts the user to insert a new bubble under a* parent *window. To do so, the user must pick a* fromBubble *and a* toBubble, *so that the new bubble can be inserted in between.*}

begin
if gotNoData **then**
    path := main
else

    {*Prompt the user to pick the* fromBubble:}
    begin
    pickBubble (parent, picked, prior);
    fromBubble := picked;

    {*If the user chooses to insert at the beginning:*}
    if fromBubble = **nil then**

        {*Prompt the user to pick the* toBubble:}
        begin
        pickBubble (parent, picked, prior);
        toBubble := picked;
        if toBubble = **nil then**
           path := notFound
        else if prior = **nil and** toBubble↑.altProcess = **nil then**
           path := main
        else
           path := notFound
        end

    {*Otherwise it is an insertion between two bubbles or at the end of a chain of bubbles:*}
    else

        {*Find the first child and last child of the parent process:*}
        begin
        firstSibling := firstOf (fromBubble↑.ownParent);
        lastSibling := lastOf (fromBubble↑.ownParent);

Figure 7.26 Algorithm for Inserting a Bubble
into a DeMarco-like Task Diagram
(Part 1 of 5)

{If it is an insertion at the end of a chain, then make sure there is no side path:}
if fromBubble↑.nextProcess = **nil then**
   if firstSibling↑.altProcess = **nil then**
     begin
     toBubble := **nil**;
     path := main
     end
   else
     path := notFound

{Otherwise it is an insertion between two bubbles:}
else

   {Prompt the user to pick the toBubble:*}*
   begin
   pickBubble (parent, picked, prior);
   toBubble := picked;

   {Determine whether the bubble should be on a main path, side path or mixed path (i.e., a side path within a main path):}
   if toBubble = fromBubble↑.nextProcess **then**
     path := main
   else if fromBubble = firstSibling
   and toBubble = lastSibling
   and fromBubble↑.firstChild = **nil**
   and toBubble↑.firstChild = **nil**
   and fromBubble↑.altProcess = toBubble **or nil then**
     path := side
   else
     begin
     process := fromBubble↑.nextProcess;
     while process ≠ toBubble **and** ≠ **nil do**
       process := process↑.nextProcess;

**Figure 7.26 Algorithm for Inserting a Bubble
into a DeMarco-like Task Diagram
(Part 2 of 5)**

```
            if process = nil then
                path := notFound
            else
                path := mixed
            end
        end
    end
end;

if path = notFound then
    write abortMessage

{If it is a mixed path, then create a group process:}
else if path = mixed then
    begin
    parent := fromBubble↑.ownParent;
    new (groupProcess);
    if fromBubble = parent↑.ownChild then
        parent↑.ownChild := groupProcess
    else
        prior↑.nextProcess := groupProcess;
    with groupProcess do
        begin
        procName := "Untitled";
        ownTaskType := parent↑.ownTaskType;
        initBubble (groupProcess);
        linkedToChild := true;
        ownChild := fromBubble;
        nextProcess := toBubble↑.nextProcess;
        ownParent := parent;
        inEvent := fromBubble↑.inEvent;
        inEventType := fromBubble↑.inEventType;
        outEvent := toBubble↑.outEvent;
        outEventType := toBubble↑.outEventType
        end
    end
```

Figure 7.26 Algorithm for Inserting a Bubble
into a DeMarco-like Task Diagram
(Part 3 of 5)

{Having determined the fromBubble *and* toBubbles *as well as the path, it is now the time to start the actual insertion process:}*
else

    {First of all, prompt the user for the location of the new bubble:}
    begin
    readMouse (point);

    {Create a new process:}
    if gotNoData **then**
       begin
       gotNoData := false;
       process := root
       end
    else
       new (process);
    with process↑ **do**
       begin
       read procName;
       initBubble (process);

       {If the new process is the root of the task diagram, then prompt the user to enter the details of input and output events:}
       if process = root **then**
          begin
          ownParent := **nil**;
          nextProcess := **nil**;
          getEventInfo (inEvent);
          getEventInfo (outEvent)
          end

       {Otherwise check whether it is an insertion in the main path:}
       else if path = main **then**
          begin
          nextProcess := toBubble;

**Figure 7.26 Algorithm for Inserting a Bubble
into a DeMarco-like Task Diagram
(Part 4 of 5)**

{*If the process is the first child of the parent, then prompt the user to enter the details of the input event, and capture the details of the output event from the* toBubble:}

```
if fromBubble = nil then
    begin
    ownParent := toBubble↑.ownParent;
    ownParent↑.ownChild := process;
    getEventInfo (inEvent);
    outEvent := toBubble↑.inEvent;
    end
```

{*Otherwise prompt the user to enter the details of the output event, and capture the details of the input event from the* fromBubble:}

```
else
    begin
    ownParent := fromBubble↑.ownParent;
    fromBubble↑.nextProcess := process;
    getEventInfo (outEvent);
    inEvent := fromBubble↑.outEvent;
    if toBubble ≠ nil then
        toBubble↑.inEvent := outEvent
    end
    end
```

{*Otherwise it is an insertion in a side path or mixed path. The treatment is similar to the above and hence will not be shown here.*}

```
else
    . . .
    end;
```

{*Draw the new bubble and link it to the* fromBubble *and* toBubbles, *if any:*}

```
bubbleTo (process)
    end
end;
```

**Figure 7.26 Algorithm for Inserting a Bubble
into a DeMarco-like Task Diagram
(Part 5 of 5)**

```
procedure cutBubble (parent):
{This is a procedure in the DeMarco program which prompts the user to delete a
bubble under a parent window.}

{First of all, prompt the user to pick the bubble to delete:}
begin
pickBubble (parent, picked, prior);
if picked = nil then
    write abortMessage
else if picked↑.ownChild = nil then
    write abortMessage
else with picked↑ do
    begin
    firstSibling := firstOf (ownParent);

    {If the user chooses to delete the first child of a parent, then change the parent
    pointer:}
    if picked = firstSibling then
        begin
        if nextProcess = nil then
            begin
            if parent↑.linkedToChild := true then
                parent↑.linkedToChild := false
            else
                shutWindow;
            parent↑.ownChild := nil
            end
        else if altProcess = nil then
            parent↑.ownChild := nextProcess
        else
            write abortMessage
        end
```

Figure 7.27 Algorithm for Deleting a Bubble
from a DeMarco-like Task Diagram
(Part 1 of 2)

{*Otherwise if the user chooses to delete the last child of a parent, then change the pointer of the previous process:*}
else if nextProcess = **nil then**
    begin
    if firstSibling↑.altProcess = **nil then**
        prior↑.nextProcess := **nil**
    else if picked = firstSibling↑.altProcess **then**
        firstSibling↑.altProcess := **nil**
    else if picked = firstSibling↑.nextProcess **then**
        with firstSibling↑ **do**
            begin
            nextProcess := altProcess;
            outEvent := nextProcess↑.inEvent;
            altProcess := **nil**
            end
    else
        write abortMessage
    end

{*Otherwise if the user chooses to delete a process in the middle of a side path, then change the pointer of the first sibling:*}
else if picked = firstSibling↑.altProcess **then**
    if picked↑.nextProcess = firstSibling↑.nextProcess **then**
        firstSibling↑.altProcess = **nil**
    else
        firstSibling↑.altProcess := nextProcess

{*Otherwise it is the deletion of a process in the middle of a main path. In this case, change the prior pointer:*}
else
    begin
    prior↑.nextProcess := nextProcess;
    prior↑.outEvent := outEvent;
    end
    end
end;

**Figure 7.27 Algorithm for Deleting a Bubble
from a DeMarco-like Task Diagram
(Part 2 of 2)**

procedure drawSubTree (parent):
{*This is a procedure in the* Transform *program which maps the task structure headed by a* parent *process into a Yourdon structure chart.*}

{*First of all, draw the parent box:*}
begin
boxTo (parent);
firstSibling := firstOf (parent);
lastSibling := lastOf (parent);

{*If there is any child under the parent process then do the following:*}
if firstSibling ≠ **nil then**

   {*If there is a side path (i.e. the task is not a sequence), then do not print the first child:*}
   begin
   if firstSibling↑.altProcess = **nil then**

      {*Otherwise if the first sibling is linked to its own children, then draw its tree:*}
      if firstSibling↑.linkedToChild **then**
         drawSubTree (firstSibling)

      {*Otherwise draw a box for the first sibling and a line linking it to the parent box:*}
      else boxTo (firstSibling);

   {*Continue to draw all the siblings under the same parent:*}
   if firstSibling↑.nextProcess ≠ **nil then**
      begin
      process := firstSibling↑.nextProcess;
      while process ≠ lastSibling **do**

         {*For each sibling, if it is linked to its own children, then draw its tree:*}
         begin
         if process↑.linkedToChild **then** drawSubTree (process)

         {*Otherwise draw a box for the sibling and a line linking it to the parent box:*}
         else boxTo (process);

**Figure 7.28 Algorithm for Drawing a Yourdon Structure Chart
(Part 1 of 2)**

```
            process := process↑.nextProcess
            end
        end;
```

{*If the task is not a sequence, then do not print the last child:*}
if firstSibling↑.altProcess = **nil then**

      {*Otherwise if there is any child under the last sibling, then draw the tree of the last sibling:*}
      begin
      if lastSibling ≠ firstSibling **and** ≠ **nil then**
         if lastSibling↑.linkedToChild **then**
            drawSubTree (lastSibling)

         {*Otherwise draw a box for the first sibling and a line linking it to the parent box:*}
         else boxTo (lastSibling)
      end

{*If there is a side path, then draw it as a branch of the tree:*}
else
      begin
      process := firstSibling↑.altProcess;
      while process ≠ lastSibling **do**

         {*For each sibling on the side path, if it is linked to its own children, then draw its tree:*}
         begin
         if process↑.linkedToChild **then**
            drawSubTree (process)

         {*Otherwise draw a box for the process and a line linking it to the parent box:*}
         else boxTo (process);
         process := process↑.nextProcess
         end
      end
    end
end;

Figure 7.28 Algorithm for Drawing a Yourdon Structure Chart
(Part 2 of 2)

```
procedure algebra (parent, level, path):
{This is a procedure in the Transform program which maps the task structure headed
by a parent process into a term algebra.}

{First of all, find the first child and last child of the parent process:}
begin
firstSibling := firstOf (parent);
lastSibling := lastOf (parent);
skip := false;
with parent↑ do
   begin

      {If the parent process is the first or last child of the grandparent, then do not print
      it:}
      if parent ≠ root then
         begin
         firstUncle := firstOf (ownParent);
         lastUncle := lastOf (ownParent);
         if firstUncle↑.altProcess ≠ nil
         and parent = firstUncle or lastUncle then
            skip := true
         end;

      {Otherwise print the parent's name and input events:}
      if skip = false then
         begin
         write ("proc (", procName, "; ");
         if moreInEvent then
            for each inEvent do
               begin
               case inEventType of
                  data: write "indata (";
                  flag: write "inflag (";
                  file: write "infile (";
                  source: write "source ("
                  end;
               if moreInEvent then
                  write (inEvent, ") + ")
               else write (inEvent, "); ")
```

Figure 7.29 Algorithm for Transforming a Task Structure
into a Term in the Initial Algebra
(Part 1 of 3)

```
                     end
        else write ''nil; '';

        {Similarly for output events:}
        . . .;

        {Print also the type of the task with the appropriate indentation:}
        if firstSibling = nil then
            write ''elem''
        else
            begin
            newLine;
            for i := 1 to level do write tab;
            if firstSibling↑.altProcess = nil then
                write ''sequ (''
            else case procType of
                seln: write ''seln ('';
                iter: write ''iter ('';
                para: write ''para (''
                end
            end
        end;

        {Continue downwards for the children of the parent process:}
        if firstSibling ≠ nil then
            begin
            algebra (firstSibling, level + 1, main);
            if firstSibling↑.nextProcess ≠ nil then
                begin
                process := firstSibling↑.nextProcess;
                while process ≠ lastSibling do
                    begin
                    algebra (process, level + 1, main);
                    process := process↑.nextProcess
                    end
                end;
            if firstSibling↑.altProcess ≠ lastSibling and ≠ nil then
                begin
                process := firstSibling↑.altProcess;
```

**Figure 7.29 Algorithm for Transforming a Task Structure
into a Term in the Initial Algebra
(Part 2 of 3)**

```
        while process ≠ lastSibling do
            begin
            algebra (process, level + 1, side);
            process := process↑.nextProcess
            end
        end;
    if lastSibling ≠ firstSibling and ≠ nil then
        algebra (lastSibling, level + 1, main)
    end;


{If the parent process is the root then do nothing:}
if parent = root then { }


{Otherwise further syntax editing is required.  In particular, if the parent is the
last child of the grandparent, then write closing brackets:}
else if parent = lastUncle then
    write "))"


{Otherwise write a semicolon and indent the next line as appropriate:}
else
    begin
    skip := false;
    if parent = firstUncle and altProcess ≠ nil then
        skip := true;
    if nextProcess = lastUncle and path = side then
        skip := true;
    if nextProcess = lastUncle and path = main
    and lastUncle = firstUncle↑.altProcess then
        skip := true;
    if skip := false then
        begin
        write ";";
        newLine;
        for i := 1 to level do write tab
        end
    end
    end
end;
```

**Figure 7.29 Algorithm for Transforming a Task Structure
into a Term in the Initial Algebra
(Part 3 of 3)**

procedure Jackson (parent, level):
{*This is a procedure in the* Transform *program which maps the task structure headed by a* parent *process into Jackson structure text.*}

begin
firstSibling := firstOf (parent);
lastSibling := lastOf (parent);

{*If the task is a sequence and the parent has only one child, then skip one level and proceed downwards:*}
if firstSibling↑.altProcess = **nil**
and firstSibling ≠ lastSibling **and** ≠ **nil then**
   Jackson (firstSibling, level)

{*Otherwise print the name of the parent with the relevant indentation:*}
else with parent↑ **do**
   begin
   for i := 1 **to** level **do** write tab;
   write procName;
   if firstSibling = **nil then**
      begin
      write ";";
      newLine
      end
   else

      {*Print also the type of the task as appropriate. Note that if the task is not a sequence, then skip the first child. Also if the task is a parallelism, then print it as seq in Jackson.*}
      begin
      if firstSibling↑.altProcess = **nil then**
         begin
         write " seq";
         newLine;
         Jackson (firstSibling, level + 1)
         end

**Figure 7.30 Algorithm for Transforming a Task Structure
into Jackson Structure Text
(Part 1 of 3)**

```
else
    begin
    case procType of
        seln: write " sel";
        iter: write " itr";
        para: write " seq"
        end;
    newLine
    end;
```

{*In any case, continue with the other children:*}
```
if firstSibling↑.nextProcess ≠ nil then
    begin
    process := firstSibling↑.nextProcess;
    while process ≠ lastSibling do
        begin
        Jackson (process, level + 1);
        process := process↑.nextProcess
        end
    end;
```

{*If the task is not a sequence, then skip the last child:*}
```
if firstSibling↑.altProcess = nil then
    begin
    if firstSibling ≠ lastSibling then
        Jackson (lastSibling, level + 1)
    end
```

{*If there are children on the side path, then print them. In particular, if the parent is a selection, then print also an* alt *line:*}
```
else if firstSibling↑.altProcess ≠ lastSibling then
    begin
    if procType = seln then
        begin
        for i := 1 to level do write tab;
        write (procName, " alt");
        newLine
        end;
```

**Figure 7.30 Algorithm for Transforming a Task Structure
into Jackson Structure Text
(Part 2 of 3)**

```
        process := firstSibling↑.altProcess;
        while process ≠ lastSibling do
           begin
           Jackson (process, level + 1);
           process := process↑.nextProcess
           end
        end;

    {Print the name of the parent again on an end line:}
    for i := 1 to level do write tab;
    write (procName, " end");
    if parent ≠ nil then
        write ";";
    newLine
        end
    end
end;
```

**Figure 7.30 Algorithm for Transforming a Task Structure
into Jackson Structure Text
(Part 3 of 3)**

8 Conclusion

Structured systems development methodologies have been recognized as the most popular tools in information systems development. They are widely accepted by practising systems developers because of the top down nature of the methodologies and the graphical nature of the tools. Unfortunately, however, the models are only derived from the experience of the authors. In spite of the popularity of these models, relative little work has been done in providing a theoretical framework to them. In this project, we have tried to solve the problem by defining a unifying theoretical framework behind the popular structured models.

We have defined an initial algebra of structured systems, which can be mapped by unique homomorphisms to a DeMarco algebra of data flow diagrams, a Yourdon algebra of structure charts and a Jackson algebra of structure texts (with equations). As a result, specifications can be transformed from one form to another. Algebraic interpreters may be adapted to validate the specifications.

We have also found that the proposed term algebra as well as the DeMarco, Yourdon and Jackson notations fit nicely into a functorial framework. The framework provides a theoretical basis for manipulating incomplete or unstructured specifications through the concepts of structured tasks and refinement morphisms. Moreover, DeMarco data flow diagrams can be mapped to term algebras through free functors. Conversely, specifications in term algebras can be mapped to other notations such as Yourdon structure charts by means of functors.

As a further illustration of the theoretical usefulness of the concept of tasks, we have derived à single criterion which is necessary and sufficient to identify unstructuredness. Namely, a connected task is unstructured if and only if there exist partially overlapping skeletons. As a straightforward corollary, we can also conclude that the absence of partially overlapping skeletons is necessary and sufficient for proving a task to be structured. The theorems are also useful for proving the structuredness of programs in general.

As an illustration of the practical usefulness, we have developed a prototype system to implement the structured tasks. It enables users to draw a hierarchy of DeMarco data flow diagrams, review them to an appropriate level of detail, and zoom in/zoom out to lower/higher levels when required. It stores the data flow diagrams internally as structured tasks, and then transforms them automatically into Yourdon structure charts and Jackson structure texts. The system has been implemented on a Macintosh using

Turbo Pascal.

We have compared our approach with other projects of a similar nature. We have found that a formal or mathematical framework is usually taken as the starting point of the other projects. The interface language would be unfamiliar to users and would therefore create a psychological distance between the users and the development tools. Our approach differs from the other projects in that an existing set of popular specification languages, namely the structured systems development models, have been chosen as the starting point of the study. A mathematical framework is built on a set of interface languages which have proven popularity and success in systems development. The formalism remains transparent to users because interaction with the system is done through a graphics workstation using the original DeMarco notations.

Bibliography

A Study Guide for Accurately Defined Systems (1969), NCR, London.

Inside Macintosh (1985), Vols. I–IV, Addison-Wesley, Reading, Massachusetts.

Turbo Pascal for the Mac: User's Guide and Reference Manual (1986), Borland, Scotts Valley, California.

PSL/PSA Introduction (1987), MetaSystems Ltd.

AHO, A.V., HOPCROFT, J.E., AND ULLMAN, J.D. (1983): *Data Structures and Algorithms*, Addison-Wesley, Reading, Massachusetts.

ALFORD, M.W. (1977): "A requirements engineering methodology for real-time processing requirements", *IEEE Transactions on Software Engineering* **SE-3** (1): 60–69.

ALFORD, M.W. (1980): "The software requirements methodology (SREM) at the age of four", in *Proceedings of 4th International Software and Applications Conference (COMPSAC '80)*, IEEE Computer Society, New York, pp. 866–874.

ALFORD, M.W. (1982): "Software requirements engineering methodology (SREM) at the age of two", in *Advanced System Development / Feasibility Techniques*, J.D. Couger, M.A. Colter and R.W. Knapp (eds.), Wiley, New York, pp. 385–393.

ALFORD, M.W. (1985): "SREM at the age of eight: the distributed computing design system", *IEEE Computer* **18** (4): 36–46.

ALTER, S. (1979): "A model for automating file and program design in business application systems", *Communications of the ACM* **22** (6): 345–353.

ARBIB, M.A. AND MANES, E.G. (1975): *Arrows, structures and functors: the categorical imperative*, Academic Press, New York.

BARR, M. AND WELLS, C. (1990): *Category Theory for Computing Science*, Prentice-Hall, Englewood Cliffs, New Jersey.

BECERRIL, J.L., BONDIA, J., CASAJUANA, R., AND VALER, F. (1980): "Grammar characterization of flowgraphs", *IBM Journal of Research and Development* **24** (6): 756–763.

BIGGERSTAFF, T.J. (1979): "The unified design specification system (UDS^2)", in *Proceedings of Conference on Specifications of Reliable Software*, IEEE Computer Society, New York, pp. 104–118.

BOEHM, B.W. (1976): "Software Engineering", *IEEE Transactions on Computers* **C-25** (12): 1226–1241.

BOEHM, B.W. (1983): "Seven basic principles of software engineering", *Journal of Systems and Software Science*, Elsevier Science **3**: 3–24.

BURSTALL, R.M. AND GOGUEN, J.A. (1980): "The semantics of Clear, a specification language", in *Abstract Software Specifications*, D. Bjorner (ed.), Lecture Notes in Computer Science, Vol. 86, Springer-Verlag, Berlin, pp. 292–332.

BURSTALL, R.M. AND GOGUEN, J.A. (1981): "An informal introduction to specifications using Clear", in *The Correctness Problem in Computer Science*, R.S. Boyer and J.S. Moore (eds.), Academic Press, London, pp. 185–213.

BURSTALL, R.M. AND GOGUEN, J.A. (1982): "Algebras, theories and freeness: an introduction for computer scientists", in *Theoretical Foundations of Programming Methodology*, M. Broy and G. Schmidt (eds.), Reidel Publishing, Dordrecht, Holland.

CAMERON, J.R. (1986): "An overview of JSD", *IEEE Transactions on Software Engineering* **SE-12** (2): 222–240.

CARDENAS, A.F. (1973): "Evaluation and selection of file organization: a model and system", *Communications of the ACM* **16** (9): 540–548.

CHEN, P.P. (1976): "The entity-relationship model: towards a unified view of data", *ACM Transactions on Database Systems* **1** (1): 9–36.

COHEN, B., HARWOOD, W.T., AND JACKSON, M.I. (1986): *The Specification of Complex Systems*, Addison-Wesley, Wokingham, U.K..

COLTER, M.A. (1982): "Evolution of the structured methodologies", in *Advanced System Development / Feasibility Techniques*, J.D. Couger, M.A. Colter and R.W. Knapp (eds.), Wiley, New York, pp. 73–96.

COLTER, M.A. (1984): "A comparative examination of systems analysis techniques", *MIS Quarterly* **10** (1): 51–66.

COLTER, M.A. (1985): "Techniques for understanding unstructured code", in *Proceedings of 6th International Conference on Information Systems*, Indianapolis, Indiana, pp. 70–88.

COWELL, D.F., GILLES, D.F., AND KAPOSI, A.A. (1980): "Synthesis and structural analysis of abstract programs", *The Computer Journal* **23** (3): 243–247.

DAVIS, A.M. (1982): "The design of a family of application-oriented requirements languages", *IEEE Computer* **15** (5): 21–28.

DAVIS, C.G. AND VICK, C.R. (1977): "The software development system", *IEEE Transactions on Software Engineering* **SE-3** (1): 69–84.

DEMARCO, T. (1978): *Structured Analysis and Systems Specification*, Yourdon Press Computing Series, Prentice-Hall, Englewood Cliffs, New Jersey.

DEMARCO, T. AND SOCENEANTU, A. (1984): "SYNCRO: a data flow command shell for the Lilith/Modula computer", in *Proceedings of 7th International Conference on Software Engineering*, New York, pp. 207–213.

DELISLE, N.M., MENICOSY, D.E., AND KERTH, N.L. (1982): "Tools for supporting structured analysis", in *Automated Tools for Information System Design*, H.-J. Schneider and A.I. Wasserman (eds.), North-Holland, Amsterdam, pp. 11–20.

DICKOVER, M.E., MCGOWEN, C.L., AND ROSS, D.T. (1978): "Software design using SADT", in *Structured Analysis and Design*, Vol. 2, State of the Art Report, Infotech, Maidenhead, U.K., pp. 99–114.

EHRIG, H. AND MAHR, B. (1985): *Fundamentals of Algebraic Specifications 1: Equations and Initial Semantics*, EATCS Monographs on Theoretical Computer Science, Springer-Verlag, Berlin.

FERGUS, R.M. (1969): "Decision tables: what, why and how", in *Proceedings of College and University Machine Records Conference*, University of Michigan, Michigan, pp. 1–20.

FERNANDEZ, C. (1975): "Net topology I", Internal Report ISF-75-9, Institut fur Informationssystem-Forschung, Gesellschaft fur Mathematik und Datenverarbeitung, Bonn.

FERNANDEZ, C. (1976): "Net topology II", Internal Report ISF-76-2, Institut fur Informationssystem-Forschung, Gesellschaft fur Mathematik und Datenverarbeitung, Bonn.

FUTATSUGI, K., GOGUEN, J.A., JOUANNAUD, J.-P., AND MESEGUER, J. (1985): "Principles of OBJ2", in *Proceedings of 12th ACM Symposium on Programming Languages*, B. Reid (ed.), ACM, pp. 52–66.

GALLIMORE, R.M., COLEMAN, D., AND STAVRIDOU, V. (1989): "UMIST OBJ: a language for executable program specifications", *The Computer Journal* **32** (5): 413–421.

GANE, C.P. AND SARSON, T. (1979): *Structured Systems Analysis: Tools and Techniques*, Prentice-Hall, Englewood Cliffs, New Jersey.

GENRICH, H.J., LAUTENBACH, K., AND THIAGARAJAN, P.S. (1980): "Elements of general net theory", in *Net Theory and Applications*, W. Brauer (ed.), Lecture Notes in Computer Science, Vol. 84, Springer-Verlag, Berlin, pp. 21–163.

GOGUEN, J.A., THATCHER, J.W., WAGNER, E.G., AND WRIGHT, J.B. (1973): "A junction between computer science and category theory, I: Basic definitions and examples, Part 1", Research Report RC-4526, IBM T.J. Watson Research Centre, Yorktown Heights, New York.

GOGUEN, J.A., THATCHER, J.W., WAGNER, E.G., AND WRIGHT, J.B. (1975): "An introduction to categories, algebraic theories and algebras", Research Report RC-5369, IBM T.J. Watson Research Center, Yorktown Heights, New York.

GOGUEN, J.A., THATCHER, J.W., WAGNER, E.G., AND WRIGHT, J.B. (1976): "A junction between computer science and category theory, I: Basic definitions and examples, Part 2", Research Report RC-5908, IBM T.J. Watson Research Centre, Yorktown Heights, New York.

GOGUEN, J.A., THATCHER, J.W., WAGNER, E.G., AND WRIGHT, J.B. (1977): "Initial algebraic semantics and continuous algebras", *Journal of the ACM* **24** (1): 68–95.

GOGUEN, J.A., THATCHER, J.W., WAGNER, E.G., AND WRIGHT, J.B. (1978): "An initial algebraic approach to specification, correctness and implementation of abstract data types", in *Current Trends in Programming Methodology*, Vol. IV: *Data Structuring*, R.T. Yeh (ed.), Prentice-Hall, Englewood Cliffs, New Jersey, pp. 80–149.

GOGUEN, J.A. AND TARDO, J.J. (1979): "An introduction to OBJ: a language for writing and testing formal algebraic program specifications", in *Proceedings of Conference on Specifications of Reliable Software*, IEEE Computer Society, New

York, pp. 170–189.

GOGUEN, J.A. (1989): "Memories of ADJ", *Bulletin of European Association for Theoretical Computer Science* (39), pp. 97–102.

GOGUEN, J.A., WINKLER, T., MESEGUER, J., FUTATSUGI, K., AND JOUANNAUD, J.-P. (1990): "Introducing OBJ3", in *Applications of Algebraic Specification using OBJ*, J.A. Goguen, D. Coleman and R.M. Gallimore (eds.), Cambridge University Press, Cambridge.

GOLDBLATT, R. (1984): *Topoi: the Categorial Analysis of Logic*, North-Holland, Amsterdam.

GREIBACH, S.A. (1975): *Theory of Program Structures: Schemes, Semantics, Verification*, Lecture Notes in Computer Science, Vol. 36, Springer-Verlag, Berlin.

HAMILTON, M. AND ZELDIN, S. (1983): "The functional life cycle model and its automation: USE.IT", *Journal of Systems and Software Science* **3** (3): 25–62.

JACKSON, M.A. (1975): *Principles of Program Design*, Academic Press, London.

JACKSON, M.A. (1983): *System Development*, Prentice-Hall, Englewood Cliffs, New Jersey.

JONES, C. (1979): "A survey of programming design and specification techniques", in *Proceedings of Conference on Specifications of Reliable Software*, IEEE Computer Society, New York, pp. 91–103.

KAMPEN, G.R. (1982): "SWIFT: a requirements specification system for software", in *Requirements Engineering Environments*, Y. Ohno (ed.), North-Holland, Amsterdam, pp. 77–84.

KENNEDY, J.F. (1961): *Inaugural Address*.

KNUTH, D.E. (1974): "Structured programming with go to statements", *ACM Computing Surveys* **6**: 261–301.

KOSARAJU, S.R. (1974): "Analysis of structured programs", *Journal of Computer and System Sciences* **9**: 232–255.

LAMB, S.S., LECK, V.G., PETERS, L.J., AND SMITH, G.L. (1978): "SAMM: a modeling tool for requirements and design specification", in *Proceedings of 2nd International Computer Software and Applications Conference (COMPSAC '78)*, IEEE Computer Society, New York, pp. 48–53.

LAUBER, R.J. (1982): "Development support systems", *IEEE Computer* **15** (5): 36–46.

MARTIN, J. (1983): *Program Design which is Provably Correct*, Savant Institute, Lancaster.

MARTIN, J. (1984): *An Information Systems Manifesto*, Prentice-Hall, Englewood Cliffs, New Jersey.

MCCABE, T.J. (1976): "A complexity measure", *IEEE Transactions on Software Engineering* **SE-2** (4): 308–320.

MCMENAMIN, S.M. AND PALMER, J.F. (1984): *Essential Systems Analysis*, Yourdon Press Computing Series, Prentice-Hall, Englewood Cliffs, New Jersey.

MESEGUER, J. AND GOGUEN, J.A. (1985): "Initiality, induction and computability", in *Algebraic methods in Semantics*, M. Nivat and J.C. Reynolds (eds.), Cambridge University Press, Cambridge, pp. 459–541.

MILLS, H.D. (1972): "Mathematical foundations for structured programming", Report FSC 72-6012, IBM Federal Systems Division, Gaithersburg, Maryland.

NUNAMAKER, J.F. (1971): "A methodology for the design and optimization of information processing systems", in *Proceedings of AFIPS Conference*, Vol. 38, pp. 283–293.

NUNAMAKER, J.F. AND KONSYNSKI, B.R. (1976): "Computer-aided analysis and design of information system", *Communications of the ACM* **19** (12): 674–687.

ORR, K.T. (1977): *Structured Systems Development*, Yourdon Press Computing Series, Prentice-Hall, Englewood Cliffs, New Jersey.

OULSMAN, G. (1982): "Unravelling unstructured programs", *The Computer Journal* **25** (3): 379–387.

PAGE-JONES, M. (1988): *The Practical Guide to Structured Systems Design*, Yourdon Press Computing Series, Prentice-Hall, Englewood Cliffs, New Jersey.

PARNAS, D.L. (1985): "Software aspects of strategic defense systems", *American Scientist* **73**: 432–440.

PETERS, L.J. AND TRIPP, L.L. (1978): "A model of software engineering", in *Proceedings of 3rd International Conference on Software Engineering*, Atlanta, Georgia, pp. 63–70.

PETERSON, J.L. (1981): *Petri Net Theory and the Modeling of Systems*, Prentice-Hall, Englewood Cliffs, New Jersey.

PRATHER, R.E. AND GIULIERI, S.G. (1981): "Decomposition of flowchart schemata", *The Computer Journal* **24** (3): 258–262.

REICHEL, H. (1987): *Initial Computability, Algebraic Specifications and Partial Algebras*, Oxford University Press, Oxford.

REISIG, W. (1984): *A Petri Net Primer*, EATCS Monographs on Theoretical Computer Science, Springer-Verlag, Berlin.

ROCK-EVANS, R. (ED.) (1987): *Analyst Workbenches*, State of the Art Report, Infotech Pergamon, Maidenhead, U.K..

ROSS, D.T. AND SCHOMAN, K.E. (1977): "Structured analysis for requirements definition", *IEEE Transactions on Software Engineering* **SE-3** (1): 6–15.

ROSS, D.T. (1977): "Structured analysis (SA): a language for communicating ideas", *IEEE Transactions on Software Engineering* **SE-3** (1): 16–34.

ROSS, D.T. (1980): "Principles behind the RSA language", in *Software Engineering*, H. Freeman and P.M. Lewis II (eds.), Academic Press, New York, pp. 159–175.

SANDEN, B. (1989): "The case for eclectic design of real-time software", *IEEE Transactions on Software Engineering* **15** (3): 360–362.

SANNELLA, D.T. (1984): "A set-theoretic semantics for Clear", *Acta Informatica* **21**: 443–472.

SCHEFFER, P.A. AND RZEPKA, W.E. (1984): "A large system evaluation of SREM", in *Proceedings of 7th International Conference on Software Engineering*, pp. 172–180.

SCHEFFER, P.A., STONE, A., AND RZEPKA, W.E. (1985): "A case study of SREM", *IEEE Computer* **18** (4): 47–54.

SEVERANCE, D.G. AND DUHNE, R. (1976): "A practitioner's guide to addressing algorithms", *Communications of the ACM* **19** (6): 314–325.

SEVERANCE, D.G. AND LOHMAN, G.M. (1976): "Differential files: their application to the maintenance of large databases", *ACM Transactions on Database Systems* **1** (3): 256–267.

SEVERANCE, D.G. AND CARLIS, J.V. (1977): "A practical approach to selecting record access paths", *ACM Computing Surveys* **9** (4): 259–272.

SHIGO, O., IWAMOTO, K., AND FUJIBAYASHI, S. (1980): "A software design system based on a unified design methodology", *Journal of Information Processing* **3** (3): 186–196.

STEPHENS, S.A. AND TRIPP, L.L. (1978): "Requirements expression and verification aid", in *Proceedings of 3rd International Conference on Software Engineering*, Atlanta, Georgia, pp. 101–108.

TARJAN, R. (1972): "Depth first search and linear graph algorithms", *SIAM Journal on Computing* **1** (2): 146–160.

TEICHROEW, D. (1971): "Problem statement analysis: requirements for the problem statement analyser (PSA)", ISDOS Working Paper 43, University of Michigan, Michigan.

TEICHROEW, D., MACASOVIC, P., HERSHEY, E.A. III, AND YAMAMOTO, Y. (1980): "Application of the entity-relationship approach to information processing systems modelling", in *Entity-Relationship Approach to Systems Analysis and Design*, P.P. Chen (ed.), North-Holland, Amsterdam, pp. 15–39.

TEICHROEW, D., HERSHEY, E.A. III, AND YAMAMOTO, Y. (1982): "The PSL/PSA approach to computer-aided analysis and documentation", in *Advanced System Development / Feasibility Techniques*, J.D. Couger, M.A. Colter and R.W. Knapp (eds.), Wiley, New York, pp. 330–346.

TRATTNIG, W. AND KERNER, H. (1980): "EDDA: a very-high-level programming and specification language in the style of SADT", in *Proceedings of 4th International Software and Applications Conference (COMPSAC '80)*, IEEE Computer Society, New York, pp. 436–443.

TSE, T.H. AND PONG, L. (1982): "A review of system development systems", *Australian Computer Journal* **14** (3): 99–109.

TSE, T.H. (1985): "An automation of Jackson's structured programming", *Australian Computer Journal* **17** (4): 154–162.

TSE, T.H. (1986): "Integrating the structured analysis and design models: an initial algebra approach", *Australian Computer Journal* **18** (3): 121–127.

TSE, T.H. (1987a): "Integrating the structured analysis and design models: a category-theoretic approach", *Australian Computer Journal* **19** (1): 25–31.

TSE, T.H. (1987b): "Towards a single criterion for identifying program unstructuredness", *The Computer Journal* **30** (4): 378–380.

TSE, T.H. (1987c): "The identification of program unstructuredness: a formal approach", *The Computer Journal* **30** (6): 507–511.

TSE, T.H. (1988): "Towards a unifying framework for structured systems development models", Ph.D. Thesis, University of London, London.

TSE, T.H. AND PONG, L. (1989): "Towards a formal foundation for DeMarco data flow diagrams", *The Computer Journal* **32** (1): 1–12.

TSE, T.H. AND PONG, L. (to appear): "An examination of requirements specification languages", *The Computer Journal*.

URSCHLER, G. (1975): "Automatic structuring of programs", *IBM Journal of Research and Development* **19**: 181–194.

WAGNER, E.G., THATCHER, J.W., AND WRIGHT, J.B. (1977): "Free continuous theories", Research Report RC-6906, IBM T.J. Watson Research Center, Yorktown Heights, New York.

WASSERMAN, A.I., FREEMAN, P., AND PORCELLA, M. (1983): "Characteristics of software development methodologies", in *Information Systems Design Methodologies: a Feature Analysis*, T.W. Olle, H.G. Sol and C.J. Tully (eds.), North-Holland, Amsterdam.

WATERS, S.J. (1977): "CAM 02: a structured precedence analyser", *The Computer Journal* **20** (1): 2–5.

WATERS, S.J. (1979): "Towards comprehensive specifications", *The Computer Journal* **22** (3): 195–199.

WEINBERG, V. (1980): *Structured Analysis*, Yourdon Press Computing Series, Prentice-Hall, Englewood Cliffs, New Jersey.

WILLIAMS, M.H. (1977): "Generating structured flow diagrams: the nature of unstructuredness", *The Computer Journal* **20** (1): 45–50.

WILLIAMS, M.H. AND OSSHER, H.L. (1978): "Conversion of unstructured flow diagrams to structured form", *The Computer Journal* **21** (2): 161–167.

WILLIAMS, M.H. (1982): "A comment on the decomposition of flowchart schemata", *The Computer Journal* **25** (3): 393–396.

WILLIAMS, M.H. (1983): "Flowchart schemata and the problem of nomenclature", *The Computer Journal* **26** (3): 270–276.

WILLIAMS, M.H. AND CHEN, G. (1985): "Restructuring Pascal programs containing goto statements", *The Computer Journal* **28** (2): 134–137.

WINOGRAD, T. (1979): "Beyond programming languages", *Communications of the ACM* **22** (7): 391–401.

YAMAMOTO, Y. (1981): "An approach to the generation of software life cycle support systems", Ph.D. Thesis, University of Michigan, Michigan.

YAO, S.B. (1977): "An attribute based model for database access cost analysis", *ACM Transactions on Database Systems* **2** (1): 45–67.

YAU, S.S. AND TSAI, J.J.-P. (1986): "A survey of software design techniques", *IEEE Transactions on Software Engineering* **SE-12** (6): 713–721.

YEH, R.T. AND ZAVE, P. (1980): "Specifying software requirements", *Proceedings of the IEEE* **68** (9): 1077–1085.

YOURDON, E. AND CONSTANTINE, L.L. (1979): *Structured Design: Fundamentals of a Discipline of Computer Program and Systems Design*, Yourdon Press Computing Series, Prentice-Hall, Englewood Cliffs, New Jersey.

Index